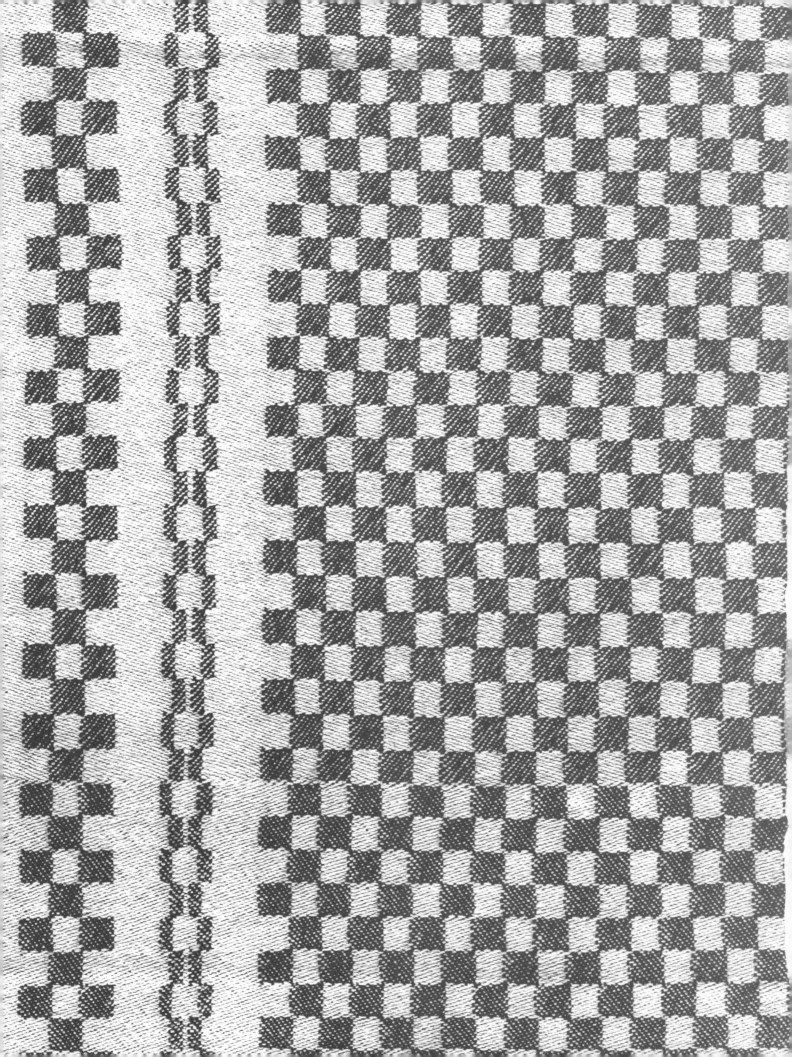

Paris Bistro Cooking

PARIS BIST

RO COOKING

by

Linda

Dannenberg

Photographs by Guy Bouchet

Design by Louise Fili and Michelle Willems

CLARKSON POTTER,
PUBLISHERS
NEW YORK

TEXT COPYRIGHT © 1991 BY LINDA DANNENBERG. PHOTOGRAPHS COPYRIGHT © 1991 BY GUY BOUCHET. ALL RIGHTS RESERVED. NO PART OF THIS BOOK MAY BE REPRODUCED OR TRANSMITTED IN ANY FORM OR BY ANY MEANS, ELECTRONIC OR MECHANICAL, INCLUDING PHOTOCOPYING, RECORDING, OR BY ANY INFORMATION STORAGE AND RETRIEVAL SYSTEM, WITHOUT PERMISSION IN WRITING FROM THE PUBLISHER. PUBLISHED BY CLARKSON N. POTTER, INC., 201 EAST 50TH STREET, NEW YORK, NEW YORK, 10022. MEMBER OF THE CROWN PUBLISHING GROUP. CLARKSON N. POTTER, POTTER AND COLOPHON ARE TRADEMARKS OF CLARKSON N. POTTER, INC.

LIBRARY OF CONGRESS CATALOGING-IN-PUBLICATION DATA   MANUFACTURED IN JAPAN

DANNENBERG, LINDA.
  PARIS BISTRO COOKING/LINDA DANNENBERG: PHOTOGRAPHS BY GUY BOUCHET—1ST ED.
    P.   CM.   INCLUDES INDEX.
  1. COOKERY, FRENCH. 2. COOKERY—FRANCE—PARIS. 3. RESTAURANTS, LUNCH ROOMS, ETC.—FRANCE—
PARIS. I. BOUCHET, GUY. II. TITLE   TX719.D24 1991   641.5944—DC20   90-47197   CIP

ISBN 0-517-57433-0

10 9 8 7 6 5 4 3 2   PART TITLE PHOTOGRAPHS © BY ED SPIRO

Dedication

TO MY PARENTS, WHOSE POST-
CARDS HOME FROM PARIS IN THE
AUTUMN OF 1953 REVEALED THE
EXISTENCE OF A MAGICAL CITY
THAT DAZZLED ME THEN, AND
DAZZLES ME STILL.

This book, long a dream of mine, was such a pleasure to write that I want to express my very first thanks to my publisher, Clarkson N. Potter, Inc., and my editors and friends within Potter and Random House—Lauren Shakely, Carol Southern, Michelle Sidrane, and Bruce Harris—for giving me the opportunity to make it a reality. I also want to thank, with no irony intended—or at least very little—the editor who rejected my proposal for a bistro cookbook in 1980. A decade ago, with another publisher, *Paris Bistro Cooking* would have been a very different book.

I am deeply grateful to the *patrons* of the Paris bistros featured in this book for opening their restaurants to me, for sharing their stories, and for providing their recipes: André Maillet of Polidor; Marc Souvrain of Chardenoux; Fernand and Jean Fleury of Le Vieux Bistro; Pierre and Colette Bardèche of Aux Charpentiers; Yves and Geneviève Cullère of La Grille; Dédée, Robert Jr., and the rest of the Collard family at L'Impasse; Paul and Andrée Launay of La Fontaine de Mars; Michel Petit of Benoît; Albert and Jean-Pierre Court of D'Chez Eux; Roger Mazarguil of Chez Georges; Elie and Hélène Bousquet of Le Restaurant Bleu; Magali, Jean, and Jean-Charles Griffoul of Au Pont Marie; Philippe Serbource of L'Auberge Pyrénées-Cévennes; Michel Rostang of Le Bistro d'à Côté; Jean Romestant and Louis Diet of La Cafetière; Jacques, Michel, and Alain Cousin of Le Petit Marguéry; Paul Racat of La Poule au Pot; Jean-François Llana of Au Chien Qui Fume; and Denise and Jacques Bénériac of La Tour de Montlhéry.

I want to offer my special thanks to Pierre Moulin and Pierre LeVec, my wonderful friends and collaborators on the Pierre Deux style books, who so generously, and so often, let me call their Paris pied-à-terre my home while I was working on this book. It made all the difference, and I am most grateful. I would also like to thank my terrific agents, Gayle Benderoff and Deborah Geltman, for helping to make each project come to life, and for their enthusiasm and support every step of the way.

For providing esoteric research information or valuable advice I would like to express my appreciation to Annick and Gregory Kerwin, Sam Lopata, and Richard Saks. For their assistance during photography sessions and the follow-up legwork, I am grateful to Monique Mourgue, Anne-Claire Picault, and Antonin Borgeaud. And for expertly testing many of the recipes, I would like to thank Ruth Cousineau and Sidney Burstein.

As always I want to express my appreciation and admiration to Guy Bouchet, friend and photographer, who comprehends my vision and renders concepts into visual poetry. And to Louise Fili and Michelle Willems, many thanks for a design that conveys the spirit of Paris.

Warmest thanks to my cherished, long-time Paris friends who shared so many bistro meals with me and enhanced each experience with their company: Esther Carliner Viros; Françoise Ledoux-Wernert; and Nivès Falcioni.

I am most grateful to my other colleagues at Clarkson N. Potter, Inc., for their participation and expertise: Howard Klein, Andrea Connolly, Catherine Sustana, Phyllis Fleiss, Jonathan Fox, Barbara Marks, Joan Denman, and Allan Eady.

Finally, a mom couldn't do this kind of work without the love, understanding, and support of her family. These gifts I get in great measure from my husband, Steve, and my son, Benjamin.

L. D.

THE TURN-OF-THE-CENTURY BAR OF CHARDENOUX WELCOMES PATRONS TO THIS CLASSIC OLD BISTRO.

LE BISTROT EST UN ÉTERNEL
POÈME, JAMAIS LE MÊME, ÉCRIT ET
RÉ-ÉCRIT MILLE FOIS PAR DES MIL-
LIERS D'AMOUREUX.

Robert Giraud, Le Point, 1960

One of the images that most exemplifies the city of Paris is that of a homey, softly lighted bistro dominated by a zinc bar and animated by agile, long-aproned waiters and a lively crowd. The cuisine is rustic, savory, inexpensive, and generously served. The atmosphere is inviting, intimate, and old-fashioned. For many visitors to Paris, the experience of bistro dining becomes one of the happiest and most cherished memories of a sojourn to this luminous city.

"A bistro is a restaurant unlike others," a lively, white-haired Parisienne named Madame Sadoul, an habitué of bistros for more than fifty years, remarked over lunch one day on the Ile-Saint-Louis. "It's not a business to make a lot of money; it's a business to enjoy people. In its most classic form—the *bistro populaire,* catering to workers and artisans—it's a simple, modest place with one person to serve and one person to cook." The definition of a bistro varies from one person to the next, but Madame Sadoul's is as good as any as a point of departure. The bistro is an intimate affair, where the owners and their employees come to know their clients well. It is not unusual in some establishments for *patrons* and clients to *tutoyer* each other—use the familiar form of address of *"tu"* rather than the more formal and polite *"vous."* Bistro is family in the broadest sense of the word, but for some habitués bistro becomes family in the narrower sense as well. In several bistros I visited, some of the clients had dined every night for decades at the same table, and for them the bistro had become a kind of surrogate home. There is a spiritual, physical comfort that is fundamental to a true bistro. It offers refuge from the outside world.

"The concept of bistro," notes Michel Petit, the chef-owner of Benoît, Paris's most luxurious bistro, "implies a certain *proximité* and even a degree of *promiscuité,* in the sense of a freeness and familiarity. The place itself should be small with a kind of homogeneity among the clientele, many of whom would know each other. Physically, many bistros have two other things in common—banquette seating and of course *un comptoir* [a bar]—primordial in this genre.''

In the course of researching this book, I asked hundreds of self-styled bistro experts—artisans, restaurateurs, bankers, professors, wine producers, civil servants, journalists—what for them were the characteristics of a real bistro. The results of this informal survey yielded the following composite sketch: It is an unpretentious neighborhood restaurant with a welcoming atmosphere, reasonable prices, and a traditional menu of home-style cooking often featuring the dishes of a particular provincial region, often the Auvergne. The core clientele is made up of habitués, usually neighbors. To this I would add that the ideal bistro for me would be chef owned and family run, with a substantial history behind it and a strong sense of tradition.

Many of today's bistros evolved from what were once called *bougnats*—small cafés operated by Auvergnats, which sold coal and wood for heating and almost as a sideline offered glasses of wine, Calvados, and coffee, and eventually rudimentary meals. The word *bougnat* derives from the first work young peasants from the Auvergne were able to find in Paris. In the late nineteenth century many Paris apartments were still not equipped with running water. To supply families with water for bathing, and earn themselves a few *sous*, hungry but hearty men trundled around small cisterns of hot water on handcarts, delivering the bath-ready water in pails to neighborhood apartments. The lowliest of work, it was the employment that fell to the dirt-poor Auvergnats in Paris, who called bathing, in their patois, *bougner* instead of the French *baigner*. The water-bearers were soon dubbed *bougnats*. A few decades later, after modern plumbing brought water into most bourgeois Paris apartments, the *bougnats* had to find another means of livelihood, and they turned to selling coal, wood, and wine. Despite their new modus vivendi the Auvergnats' little establishments continued to be known as *bougnats*, in popular slang, or alternatively as *cafés-charbons*.

The origin of the word *bistro* (also spelled *bistrot*) is more difficult to pinpoint. The commonly accepted explanation is that when Russian soldiers marched on Paris after Napoleon's defeat at Waterloo in 1815, they broke rank, rushed into the city's cabarets in search of food and drink, and called out *"Bistro! Bistro!"* (''Quick! Quick!'' in dialect). Another, more esoteric explanation is that the word evolved from the progressive slang deformation of the noun *mastroquet*, meaning publican or barkeeper, into *bistroquet, bistroque,* and finally *bistrotier*—the man who kept a *bistrot*.

Many bistros began, by necessity rather than by design, as canteens to serve workers in or near Les Halles, the sprawling market district described by Emile Zola as the ''belly'' of Paris. As their honest good cooking at fair prices gained renown beyond Les Halles's boundaries, struggling artists and journalists—too young to have wives and kitchens in their garrets—dined, debated, and virtually lived in their favorite bistros, returning night after night to familiar menus of home-style cooking. Although not imbued with the intellectual or social flavor of the cafés—after dinner it was on to the cabarets—these bistros nurtured the soul. The grandmotherly women who ran them were known as *mères*, and their fare as *cuisine de mères*. Many confidences were shared along with the evening meal at the old bistros.

The key to the bistro's allure has always been its deeply satisfying, down-to-earth cooking.

ANTIQUE LINENS CREATE A HOMEY ATMOSPHERE AT LA GRILLE.

THE DINING ROOM AT BENOÎT IS CHIC, BUT WITH OLD-FASHIONED TOUCHES.

Paris bistros offer their faithful customers food that warms the heart and pleases the palate. It is fare that might have come from the cozy kitchen of a country grandmother. Bistros feature many stews, ragouts, and baked casseroles—*boeuf bourguignon, blanquette de veau,* cassoulet, for example—dishes that can be prepared ahead of time and then ladled onto a plate and served. Roasts are another staple—a savory, garlic-studded leg of lamb; a crisp, golden roast chicken; or a rare and tender rib of beef, sliced to order and served with a *galette de pommes de terre,* a baked "pancake" of sliced potatoes, onions, and bacon. For starters there are hearty composed salads, such as the classic *frisée aux lardons,* the curly endive, crouton, and slab-bacon salad; and soups that could make meals in themselves, like the traditional *gratinée des Halles*—French onion soup with a baked cheese crust. Desserts are as straightforward and simple as the rest of the menu—big crocks of chocolate mousse; ceramic pots of *crème caramel* hiding luscious soupy caramel sauce at the bottom; slices of glowingly fresh fruit tarts that defy a dessert plate to hold them; and plates full of bright raspberries or strawberries topped with ivory mounds of crème fraîche.

To accompany this addictive fare are modest, flavorful wines often bought by the bistro *patron* directly from the vineyard, shipped in barrels, and served from a spigot at the bar. Wines are frequently in the *ça se laisse boire* category—young, light, fruity wines that "let themselves be drunk." Traditional bistro wines include Beaujolais, particularly Brouilly, Chiroubles, and Morgon; wines of the Loire such as Sancerre, Chinon, and Bourgueil; Côtes-du-Rhône such as Hermitage and Châteauneuf-du-Pape; and the more full-bodied wines of the Southwest, the rustic Cahors and Madiran. In some bistros you pay only for what you drink from bottles, filled at the bar, that need no corks.

"If you are lucky enough to have lived in Paris as a young man," Hemingway wrote at the beginning of *A Moveable Feast,* "then wherever you go for the rest of your life, it stays with you, because Paris is a moveable feast." As a young woman I was lucky enough to have lived in Paris, and Hemingway was right. Paris has stayed with me, wherever I've gone, since I was twenty-two years old and came to live on the Boulevard Exelmans and work as a *stagiaire,* a trainee, in a now-defunct fabric house. This book is an homage to the city I fell in love with that year, and which has compelled me to return every year since, often for months at a time. My happiest memories from those lovely, lost days are composed mainly of moonlight kisses on bridges over the Seine (romantic clichés are a reality in Paris), and long, late-night dinners in the lively bistros of the *quartier latin* and Les Halles. While the kisses were sweet, it was the experience of the bistros that I sought to recapture on every subsequent trip and which became, eventually, the inspiration for this book. I wanted to celebrate the special, joyous experience that is bistro dining, and record the recipes that make bistro meals outstanding. I also wanted to tell the stories of the bistros themselves, each intriguing and unique, each revealing in microcosm part of this venerable city's social history. Many of the old-time Paris bistros are, sadly, disappearing from the map of Paris. In just the two years that I worked on this project, two lovely old places—the Restaurant des Saints-Pères and Chez Rabu—closed their doors, and at least three other venerable spots told me they would be out of business by the time this book was published. It is my hope that *Paris Bistro Cooking* will be as much a book of record as it is a cookbook.

LASSIQUES

DAILY SPECIALTIES ARE STILL POSTED ON THE BLACKBOARD AT POLIDOR, AS THEY WERE IN THE TIME OF RIMBAUD.

POLIDOR

The Latin Quarter neighborhood of the rue Monsieur-le-Prince had spawned so many restaurants by the mid-1800s that Honoré Daumier, the satirical lithographer and painter, dubbed it a district of *"saucialistes."* It is still a neighborhood saturated with little restaurants, but most of those that existed in Daumier's day are long gone. Most, but not all: There remains the "Crémerie Restaurant Polidor," a historic bistro that harbors the hungry ghosts of Paris literary legend. Here poets Arthur Rimbaud and Paul Verlaine, neighbors on the rue Monsieur-le-Prince, dined as frequently as they could afford in the 1890s. A generation later it was the gathering spot for habitués like James Joyce, Ernest Hemingway when he lived on the Place de la Contrescarpe, Max Ernst, and André Gide. The small back room, sheltered between the kitchen and the main restaurant, was the preferred seating area of the literary crowd. At a table under the little room's *années folles* murals, signed "Le Fevre," writer Paul Valéry dined throughout his life.

One of the most faithful of the habitués, Valéry was given napkin drawer 2 in the old black napkin cabinet in the front room that held the linen of the regular clientele. He paid when he could, and when he couldn't the amount was chalked up on a blackboard kept for that

THE FAÇADE OF POLIDOR, FREQUENTED BY FACULTY AND STUDENTS FROM THE NEARBY SORBONNE, HAS REMAINED VIRTUALLY UNCHANGED IN 100 YEARS.

. . . .

purpose. Many artists of the day enjoyed the same generous credit policies that Polidor extended to the famous Symbolist poet.

There is nothing chic or fashionable about Polidor. It is, in fact, unabashedly shabby and old. But therein lies its allure and unique ambiance. It evokes a Paris of yesteryear, both in its ochered atmosphere and in its straightforward and inexpensive menu. Succeeding generations keep Polidor thriving. On weekend nights especially, when a cacophony of talk, laughter, and clinking cutlery makes tête-à-têtes a challenge, Polidor rivals the vitality of Paris' trendiest eateries. The crowd of students, professors from the Sorbonne, old couples, young lovers, artists, models, businessmen, writers, and tourists fills oilcloth-covered tables of two to twenty. Seated elbow to elbow, their numbers are multiplied by the big beveled mirrors set above the wooden wainscoting.

Polidor has always offered consistent good-quality and unsurprising food at extremely reasonable prices, a formula that is proven by the bistro's longevity. The faithful don't come here for innovation or fantasy. They come here for the 50-franc prix fixe menu (lunch only) that includes Assiette de Crudités (raw vegetable plate), *riz à l'andalouse* (rice salad with tomatoes and red and green peppers), or a *terrine de campagne* (a country-style terrine); a *plat du jour*, such as Petit-Salé aux Lentilles (salt pork with lentils) or *poule sauce suprême* (chicken in cream sauce); and a selection of desserts like a *baba au rhum*, Tarte au Citron (lemon tart), or a *mousse au chocolat*. And they come for the beef bourguignon, the leg of lamb, the roast chicken with cabbage, and the *truite meunière*, all served with speed and simplicity by black-garbed waitresses in white aprons.

Polidor's proprietor today—only the fourth since the turn of the century—is the entrepreneurial André Maillet, who, although he has added an ice cream parlor next to his landmark property, has vowed to maintain his much-loved restaurant in the old tradition. And an old tradition it is, dating back to 1845, when Polidor was founded by a family from Normandy as a *cré-*

merie, or dairy shop, selling milk, eggs, and cheese. By the end of the century, Polidor, like many Paris *crémeries*, had become a small, simple restaurant. In the early 1890s the handsome marble and gilt "Crémerie Restaurant Polidor" sign was hoisted above the doorway. Even older—much older—than the original *crémerie* is Polidor's cellar, the remains of the thirteenth-century ramparts constructed by Philippe-Auguste, an early king of France, to enclose and protect the Paris of the 1200s. "We'd love to renovate our old bathrooms," remarks André Maillet, "but we can't because the supporting walls are classified as historic monuments."

The antiquated bathrooms behind the little glass-and-wood door marked *Lavabos* are as much a part of Polidor's charm as the nineteenth-century tiled floor, the numbered napkin drawers, and the blackboard menus, and most diners would rebel against the least modernization. For many Parisians, as well as many foreigners who sojourned or studied in Paris as young men and women, Polidor is associated with their happiest

. . . .

PERIOD DETAILS LIKE THIS OLD DOOR HANDLE ENHANCE POLIDOR'S "OLD PARIS" ATMOSPHERE.

early years. It is why the Farah Diba, once a student at the Sorbonne, returns here from time to time for a dinner with friends; it is why one American devotee who met his wife in the back room in 1968 visits every time he comes to Paris, and has offered to pay for the repair of the aging tilework whenever it becomes necessary; and it is why the *livre d'or*, the guest book, is filled with reminiscences that extend back twenty, forty, even sixty-five years. "I dined *chez vous* more than fifty years ago," wrote French writer Michel Caron. "Your reputation was already established before I was born. I came back in 1976... nothing had changed. I rediscovered my youth, and I thank you for it."

THE MAIN INGREDIENT OF SOUPE DE POTIRON, ENRICHED WITH CRÈME FRAÎCHE, IS PUMPKIN GROWN IN SOUTHERN FRANCE.

· · · · · · · · · · · ·

Soupe de Potiron

[PUMPKIN SOUP]

3 CUPS WATER

1 MEDIUM ONION, DICED

1 TABLESPOON SUGAR

2 TEASPOONS SALT

16 OUNCES (1 CAN) PUMPKIN PUREE (UNFLAVORED)

1 CUP MILK

SALT AND FRESHLY GROUND BLACK PEPPER

SOUR CREAM OR CRÈME FRAÎCHE (OPTIONAL)

In a medium saucepan, bring the water, onion, sugar, and salt to a boil. Cover and simmer 15 minutes.

Whisk in the pumpkin. Bring to a boil, then simmer, uncovered, for 5 minutes, stirring constantly.

Puree the mixture in batches in a food processor or blender until smooth. Pour into a medium saucepan and whisk in the milk. Heat the soup to a boil, then season to taste with salt and pepper.

Serve with dollops of sour cream or crème fraîche, if desired.

MAKES ABOUT 5½ CUPS;
SERVES 4

Pintade aux Lardons et au Chou

[ROAST GUINEA HEN WITH BACON AND CABBAGE]

1 3-POUND GUINEA HEN OR CHICKEN, QUARTERED

2 MEDIUM CARROTS, SLICED

2 MEDIUM ONIONS, SLICED

2 GARLIC CLOVES, CRUSHED

1 BOUQUET GARNI (1 SPRIG OF PARSLEY, GREENS OF 1 LEEK, AND 1 BAY LEAF, TIED IN A SQUARE OF CHEESECLOTH)

2 WHOLE CLOVES

SALT AND FRESHLY GROUND BLACK PEPPER

3 TO 4 CUPS DRY WHITE WINE

5 OUNCES SLAB BACON, CUT IN THIN STRIPS 2 × ¼ INCH THICK

2 TABLESPOONS ALL-PURPOSE FLOUR

3 CUPS CHICKEN STOCK, APPROXIMATELY

2 POUNDS KALE, STEMS TRIMMED

In a large bowl, combine the guinea hen or chicken, carrots, onions, garlic, bouquet garni, and cloves. Sprinkle with salt and pepper. Cover with the wine and marinate 3 hours in a cool place.

Blanch the bacon in boiling water for 5 minutes. Remove, drain, and dry bacon. In a 5½-quart pot sauté bacon 5 to 7 minutes, stirring, until golden. Lift with a slotted spoon and reserve, leaving the oil in the pan.

Remove the chicken from the marinade and pat dry, reserving the marinade. In the pot with the oil, deeply brown the chicken for 8 minutes on each side. Remove the chicken and set aside. Pour all but 1 tablespoon of the fat from the pan. Sprinkle in the flour and cook about 1 minute, stirring. Add the reserved marinade and cook over low heat for several minutes, scraping the bottom of the pot. Stir in stock or water.

Return the chicken to the pot (the liquid should almost cover the

THE PINTADE AUX LARDONS ET AU CHOU
IS A RICH AND HEARTY ENTRÉE.

· · · · · · · · · · · ·

ZEST OF 1 ORANGE AND
1 LEMON, GRATED

2 CUPS CRÈME FRAÎCHE OR
HEAVY CREAM

3 LARGE EGGS, LIGHTLY BEATEN

· · · · · · · · · ·

CARAMEL

½ CUP SUGAR

3 TABLESPOONS WATER

A POPULAR APPETIZER *CHEZ* POLIDOR IS
THE GENEROUS CRUDITÉ PLATE.

· · · · · · · · · · · ·

chicken) and bring to a boil. Reduce the heat and simmer 30 minutes, partially covered.

Meanwhile, bring a large quantity of salted water to a boil in a large pot, add the kale, and cook for 5 minutes. Rinse, drain, and squeeze out the moisture. Carefully cut the kale crosswise into ¼-inch strips.

Add the kale and the reserved bacon strips to the chicken. Continue cooking 15 minutes or until the juices run clear. Remove bouquet garni.

Dish into 4 shallow bowls and serve immediately.

SERVES 4

Gâteau de Riz

[RICE CAKE]

· · · · · · · · · ·

CAKE

1 QUART MILK

1 CUP SHORT-GRAIN RICE

⅔ CUP SUGAR

½ CUP RAISINS, SOAKED
20 MINUTES IN ¼ CUP RUM

TO MAKE CAKE: In a heavy 5½-quart pot, stir together the milk, rice, sugar, raisins and rum, and orange and lemon zests. Heat to a simmer. Cook over low heat, stirring constantly, until the mixture is thick and the rice is soft, about 40 minutes. Be careful not to scorch. Cool to lukewarm. Preheat the oven to 350°F. Stir the crème fraîche and eggs into the rice mixture.

TO MAKE CARAMEL: Heat the sugar and the water in a small, heavy-bottomed saucepan over medium heat until the sugar caramelizes to an amber color.

Swirl the caramel on the bottom and sides of a 9½ × 5½ × 3-inch loaf pan. Pour in the rice mixture. Place the pan in a bain-marie (or a larger pan) of just-simmering water and bake for 55 to 60 minutes, until the edges are golden. Cool, then refrigerate until cold and firm to the touch.

Slice and serve with Crème Anglaise (see page 70), if desired.

MAKES AT LEAST 15 SLICES

Assiette de Crudités

[RAW VEGETABLE PLATE]

The *crudité* plate is a ubiquitous appetizer at bistros throughout France. It is composed of a varying assortment of raw vegetables in a vinaigrette sauce or mayonnaise. At Polidor the composition is shredded carrots tossed with a vin-

aigrette (4 parts olive oil to 1 part vinegar, salt, and pepper); Céleri Rémoulade (see page 79); diced beets tossed with a vinaigrette; quartered tomatoes; and a *macédoine* of vegetables (steamed cold diced carrots, cut green beans, and steamed peas) in a mustard mayonnaise. Other restaurants include thinly sliced cucumbers, seeds removed; diced cold boiled potatoes; whole baby radishes; sliced mushroom caps; celery sticks; sliced fennel; and cauliflower florets. It can be, in short, whatever colorful and crunchy assortment of vegetables you wish it to be, served always with fresh crusty bread and usually lightly salted butter.

Petit-Salé aux Lentilles

[SALT PORK WITH LENTILS]

In France, salt pork, or *petit-salé*, is made from pork belly or hock cured in brine; in the United States salt pork is usually made from pork back fat, a less meaty, fattier cut. Ask your butcher to select for you a particularly meaty piece of salt pork, or substitute a piece of cured pork belly, shoulder, or loin, if available.

· · · · · · · · · ·

SALT PORK

2 POUNDS MEATY SALT PORK, RIND REMOVED

1 LARGE ONION, STUCK WITH 2 WHOLE CLOVES

2 LARGE CARROTS

1 BOUQUET GARNI (1 SPRIG OF PARSLEY, GREENS OF 1 LEEK, THYME SPRIG, AND 1 BAY LEAF, TIED IN A SQUARE OF CHEESECLOTH)

· · · · · · · · · ·

LENTIL GARNISH

1 POUND LENTILS, CLEANED

4 MEDIUM CARROTS, QUARTERED

2 MEDIUM ONIONS, QUARTERED

1 BOUQUET GARNI (SAME AS ABOVE)

SALT AND FRESHLY GROUND PEPPER

2 TABLESPOONS CHOPPED FRESH PARSLEY

TO PREPARE THE SALT PORK: Place the salt pork, onion, carrots, and bouquet garni in a large pot. Cover with cold water and bring to a boil. Lower the heat and simmer for 2 hours, until salt pork is tender.

· · · · · · · · · · · ·

PETIT-SALÉ AUX LENTILLES IS A SPECIALTY AVAILABLE ONLY ON TUESDAYS.

TO MAKE THE LENTIL GARNISH: Place the lentils, carrots, onions, and bouquet garni in a pot and add enough water to cover the lentils by 3 inches. Bring to a boil, then simmer gently for about 1 hour.

When the salt pork is ready, drain and discard accompanying vegetables and bouquet garni. Place the salt pork in the lentils pot and simmer for 30 minutes. (Add water if necessary to prevent the lentils from drying out.) Adjust seasoning. Before serving, remove bouquet garni from lentils.

To serve, slice the salt pork, place it on top of the lentils, and sprinkle with the parsley.

SERVES 4

Tarte au Citron

[LEMON TART]

· · · · · · · · · ·

PÂTE SUCRÉ

1¾ CUPS SIFTED ALL-PURPOSE FLOUR

7 TABLESPOONS UNSALTED BUTTER, CHILLED

⅔ CUP SUGAR

2 LARGE EGGS, BEATEN WITH 2 TEASPOONS WATER

· · · · · · · · · ·

FILLING

4 TABLESPOONS FRESH LEMON JUICE

¼ CUP SUGAR

3 LARGE EGGS

¾ CUP HEAVY CREAM

ADDITIONAL SUGAR TO GLAZE, IF DESIRED

TO MAKE THE PÂTE SUCRÉ: In a large bowl, work together the flour and butter, then the sugar, and egg-and-water mixture, mixing with your fingertips. Knead to a smooth consistency. On a lightly floured surface, roll the dough into a 12- to 13-inch circle.

POLIDOR'S LUNCH-ONLY PRIX FIXE MENU FEATURES THE TANGY TARTE AU CITRON.

· · · · · · · · · · · ·

Press the dough circle into the bottom and up the sides of a 10-inch tart pan with a removable bottom, leaving ¼ inch above the rim. Chill for 30 minutes.

Preheat the oven to 375°F.

TO MAKE THE FILLING: Whisk together the lemon juice, sugar, eggs, and cream in a bowl.

Prick the side and bottom of the chilled crust with a fork. Line with a sheet of foil, pressing the foil gently against the sides and bottom, and fill with dried beans or pastry pellets. Arrange the prepared pan on a medium baking sheet. Bake for 20 minutes, removing the foil after 10 minutes and flattening the crust with a fork if puffed.

Remove the crust from the oven. Ladle the filling carefully into baked crust and return to the oven. Bake 30 to 35 minutes, until the filling is firm to the touch. Let cool on a rack.

Sprinkle with sugar to glaze, if desired. Shield the edges of the tart with foil to prevent burning and run quickly under the broiler until golden.

SERVES 6 TO 8

FROM JEREBOAM TO SPLIT, POLIDOR OFFERS A RANGE OF WINES AND CHAMPAGNES TO ITS CLIENTELE.

The romantic Art Nouveau interior of Chardenoux makes it one of the most beautiful bistros in Paris.

CHARDENOUX

*I*n an old photograph taken of Chardenoux shortly after it was founded in 1909, not only the whole staff but also what appears to be virtually the whole neighborhood gathers around tables, clusters on the curb, or stands in the doorway beneath a striking marquee that announces a mug of beer for 15 *centimes* and a telephone on the premises. The men wear their *casquettes*; the women have their hair twisted into topknots and long white aprons over their dresses; and the children wear their *tabliers*, their roomy school smocks. Laundry, as well as a French flag, hangs from the open windows above the marquee. Established by a family from Laguiole, in the Aveyron, Chardenoux was a people's bistro in a *quartier populaire*, a working-class neighborhood dominated by cabinetmakers and carpenters.

Today Chardenoux still commands the corner of the rue Jules-Vallès and the rue de Chanzy in the rapidly gentrifying 11th *arrondissement*, near the Bas-

tille. The character of the clientele and the cuisine has changed substantial-ly from the early days, but much of the period decor remains, making Char-denoux one of the most beautiful small bistros in Paris. Etched-glass pan-els separate the bar from the dining area; the hand-some celadon ceiling is

appliquéd with elaborate Belle Epoque scrollwork painted in warm toffee tones; and large beveled mirrors reflect the light from graceful wrought-iron hanging fixtures. But the high point of the interior is the magnificent, sinuous bar that leads the eye in from the double doors to the heart of the restaurant. The bar is a mélange of carved amber and pink marbles handsomely worked against a black background. The top is sleek and gleaming pewter that subtly reflects the tall spray of bright seasonal flowers set at one end in an Art Nouveau vase. Here at the bar, seated atop black bentwood stools, diners, among them the popular French cartoonist Wolinski and a number of race-car drivers on the Formula 1 circuit, enjoy an apéritif while their tables are prepared. Later on, neighbors warm the stools while nursing snifters of Armagnac until closing time.

Chardenoux is the pampered property of architect and bon vivant Marc Souvrain, who acquired the restaurant in 1986, only the third owner in the restaurant's long history. Souvrain, whose hotel commissions take him around the world, was beguiled by a totally different modus vivendi—the routine and atmosphere of a classic bistro. Chardenoux is his second foray into this world; the first was a fish restaurant, Le Turbot, near Montparnasse. "I love food, I love wine, I love entertaining," he says. "For fourteen years, while I was living in Abidjan on the Ivory Coast during the 1960s and 1970s, I held a weekly *table ouverte*—an 'open table' where I would cook for twenty or thirty people at a time— for anyone who wanted to show up." Having his own restaurant springs from this same spirit of *bonhomie*. Although he continues to work long hours on his architectural projects, he appears almost every night that he's in town at Chardenoux. "In the evening," says Souvrain, "I like leaving my drawing board and client problems behind and coming into this convivial and nostalgic little world, so different from my *métier*."

Marc Souvrain's collaborator and chef is Dominique Mazelin, a Norman from Pont L'Evêque. His cuisine is an imaginative mix of contemporary and classic dishes, some making ample use of the rich butter and cream of his native region, like his Huîtres Chaudes sur Endives (poached oysters served on a bed of sautéed endive and bathed in a cream sauce); and the Cerises à la Savoyarde (cherries Savoyard), a luscious dessert resembling cherries jubilee. Other dishes in Dominique Mazelin's repertoire are nouvelle in their fat-free purity, such as his well-known *saumon à l'unilatérale* (salmon filet grilled skin side only), and his ambrosia-like Salade d'Oranges. Many traditional bistro dishes highlight Chef Mazelin's menu as well: a crisply textured salad of endive, walnuts, and blue cheese; Oeufs en Meurette (eggs poached in red wine); a cassoulet with duck confit; a *boudin noir aux deux pommes* (blood sausage served with two kinds of *pommes:* sautéed apples [*pommes*] and a golden gratin of potatoes [*pommes de terre*]); and a wonderful, juicy Gigot à la Crème d'Ail (roast leg of lamb with garlic cream).

Dominique Mazelin, like many restaurant chefs, habitually works a long, six-day week, with only Saturday afternoons and Sundays off. To give his chef the benefit of a full weekend from time to time and still remain open on Saturday, Marc Souvrain has devised a singular solution. Two weekends a month, Souvrain takes over the kitchen himself, laying aside his pens and blueprints for the whisks and casseroles of the *cuisinier*. "I cook as though I'm making a big party for friends," he says. "I love to make old-fashioned, rustic dishes that a busy chef normally doesn't have time for, like my *gigot d'agneau de sept heures* [a large leg of lamb that roasts slowly for seven hours]. Unbelievably tender and delicious!" You don't have to be a friend to reserve a place for a Souvrain Saturday night, but if you manage to have a table at Chardenoux on one of these biweekly evenings, you will certainly feel like one.

Oeufs en Meurette

[EGGS POACHED IN RED WINE]

4 CUPS DRY RED WINE, PREFERABLY BURGUNDY (SEE NOTE)

1 BOUQUET GARNI (1 SPRIG EACH OF PARSLEY AND THYME, AND 1 BAY LEAF, TIED IN A SQUARE OF CHEESECLOTH)

1 MEDIUM ONION, STUCK WITH 1 WHOLE CLOVE

1 MEDIUM CARROT, QUARTERED

1 SMALL LEEK, WHITE ONLY

RICH AND FILLING, OEUFS EN
MEURETTE IS A VENERABLE BISTRO
APPETIZER.

. . . .

SALT AND FRESHLY GROUND
PEPPER

8 VERY FRESH, LARGE EGGS

10 OUNCES SLAB BACON, CUT IN
¼-INCH STRIPS, BLANCHED

10 TABLESPOONS (1¼ STICKS)
UNSALTED BUTTER

24 SMALL WHITE ONIONS

24 SMALL MUSHROOMS

2 TABLESPOONS ALL-PURPOSE
FLOUR

8 SLICES TOASTED FRENCH
BREAD

2 TABLESPOONS FINELY MINCED
FRESH PARSLEY

Bring the wine, bouquet garni, onion, carrot, and leek to a boil in a nonreactive saucepan, then lower the heat and simmer for 30 minutes. Strain and discard the bouquet garni and the vegetables. Bring the remaining bouillon to a simmer, season with salt and pepper to taste, and poach the eggs in the bouillon for 3 to 4 minutes. Drain the eggs on a kitchen towel and set aside, keeping warm.

Meanwhile, sauté the bacon until crisp, drain, and set aside.

Melt 3 tablespoons of the butter in a large skillet, add the small onions and mushrooms and sauté until they are tender, about 10 minutes. Set aside with the bacon.

Melt 3 tablespoons of the butter in a saucepan, whisk in the flour, and cook over low heat several minutes, stirring often. Pour in the bouillon, whisking until smooth. Cook about 8 minutes on medium heat, stirring occasionally. Beat in the remaining 4 tablespoons of the butter.

Place the eggs on the toasts on individual plates. Strew the bacon, onions, and mushrooms around the eggs, and cover with the sauce. Sprinkle with parsley.

SERVES 8

NOTE: Eggs poached in wine bouillon turn slightly purple, an unusual color for eggs upon first encounter.

Gigot à la Crème d'Ail

[LEG OF LAMB WITH
GARLIC CREAM]

At Chardenoux, the *gigot* is served with a potato *gratin*, such as the one on page 37; it is also good accompanied by any kind of haricot bean—white, red, or flageolet—boiled and buttered or in a puree.

GARLIC CREAM

6 HEADS GARLIC

2 CUPS MILK

1 BAY LEAF

SALT AND FRESHLY GROUND
PEPPER

2 CUPS HEAVY CREAM

. . . .

LAMB

3 POUNDS BONED LEG OF LAMB,
ALL FAT TRIMMED

3 GARLIC CLOVES, SLIVERED

½ TEASPOON DRIED THYME

½ TEASPOON DRIED ROSEMARY
OR SAVORY

FRESHLY GROUND PEPPER

2 TABLESPOONS OLIVE OIL

TO MAKE THE GARLIC CREAM: Separate the garlic but do not peel the cloves. Blanch them for 2 minutes in boiling salted water. Drain. Combine the garlic, milk, bay leaf, salt, and pepper in a medium saucepan. Cover and simmer over very low heat for 45 minutes. Strain the sauce into another pan and squeeze the garlic from the peels into the sauce. Whisk in the cream and cook over medium heat until reduced by one-third. Adjust seasonings. Sauce can be made ahead and reheated over low heat.

. . . .

DOMINIQUE MAZELIN'S *GIGOT D'AGNEAU* IS SAVORY WITH THE PROVENÇAL FLAVORS
OF ROSEMARY, THYME, AND GARLIC.

THE COMPLEMENTARY FLAVORS AND TEXTURES OF ORANGES AND CHOCOLATE
DISTINGUISH SALADE D'ORANGES AU SORBET CHOCOLAT.

. . . .

TO PREPARE THE LAMB: Preheat the oven to 500°F. Make slits all over the lamb with a sharp thin-bladed knife. Toss the garlic slivers with the dried herbs and insert into the slits in the lamb. Sprinkle pepper over the lamb and rub with the olive oil. Place the lamb on a rack in a shallow roasting pan and bake about 45 minutes for rare. Let the meat rest 5 minutes before slicing. Serve with the garlic cream.

SERVES 6

Salade d'Oranges au Sorbet Chocolat

[ORANGE SALAD WITH CHOCOLATE SORBET]

4 LARGE ORANGES, PEELED AND SECTIONED, ALL MEMBRANES REMOVED

JUICE OF 1 ORANGE

JUICE OF 1 LEMON

1 TABLESPOON GRAND MARNIER OR COINTREAU

1 ROUNDED TABLESPOON VANILLA SUGAR (SEE DIRECTORY FOR SOURCES, OR SUBSTITUTE 1 ROUNDED TABLESPOON SUGAR COMBINED WITH ½ TEASPOON VANILLA EXTRACT)

5 TABLESPOONS LIGHT CANE OR CORN SYRUP, SUCH AS KARO

ZEST OF 1 ORANGE, SHREDDED IN LONG FINE STRIPS

CHOCOLATE SORBET (SEE NOTE)

Arrange the orange sections in a wide, low glass or ceramic bowl. Pour the orange juice, lemon juice, and Grand Marnier or Cointreau over the oranges, then sprinkle with the vanilla sugar. Set aside.

In a small saucepan, combine the syrup and orange zest. Over medium heat, bring the mixture to a low boil and cook 5 minutes. Pour the boiling syrup over the oranges. Cover with plastic wrap and refrigerate overnight. Serve the salad accompanied by a small dish of chocolate sorbet.

SERVES 4

NOTE: This dessert would be equally good with an intensely flavored chocolate frozen yogurt, such as Élan, or a rich chocolate ice cream.

Huîtres Chaudes sur Endives

[POACHED OYSTERS ON A BED OF ENDIVE]

12 OYSTERS, PARTIALLY OPENED AT THE FISH STORE (LEAVING SHELLS AND OYSTER INTACT) OR SHUCKED OYSTERS PACKED IN THEIR LIQUOR

2 ENDIVE

4 TEASPOONS UNSALTED BUTTER

1 TEASPOON SUGAR

JUICE OF 1 LEMON

SALT AND FRESHLY GROUND PEPPER

½ CUP HEAVY CREAM

YOLK OF 1 LARGE EGG

4 SPRIGS PARSLEY, CHOPPED

Open the oysters and pour the liquor from the oysters through a fine sieve into a saucepan. Bring the liquor to a simmer over medium heat, then add the oysters. Cook the oysters for 1 to 2 minutes, just until they plump up. Set the oysters aside, reserving the liquor.

Cut the endive crosswise into rounds. In a frying pan, melt the butter and sauté the endive rounds. Sprinkle with the sugar and cook for an additional 2 minutes. Add the lemon juice and the salt and pepper. Cook gently for 15 minutes, until the endive is tender.

Add the cream to the reserved oyster liquor and reduce over medium-high heat until thickened, about 5 minutes. Remove the pan from the heat and whisk in the egg yolk. Season lightly with additional salt and pepper, if desired, and add the reserved oysters. Place the endive in a warm serving dish and spoon the oysters on top, then garnish with chopped parsley.

SERVES 2

ONE OF CHARDENOUX'S LIGHTER OFFERINGS IS THE POACHED *FILET DE MERLAN*
SERVED ON A BED OF VEGETABLES.

. . . .

Filet de Merlan à la Julienne de Légumes

[POACHED WHITING WITH JULIENNE VEGETABLES]

Chef Dominique Mazelin serves the *filet de merlan* accompanied by buttered white rice. Steamed basmati rice is also good with this dish.

1 POUND FISH BONES FROM THE FILETS (REQUEST BONES FROM FISH STORE WHEN BUYING FILETS)

2 TEASPOONS UNSALTED BUTTER

2 CUPS WATER, BOILING

2 CUPS DRY WHITE WINE, PREFERABLY SAUVIGNON BLANC

1 SHALLOT, HALVED

1 GARLIC CLOVE, CRUSHED

1 MEDIUM ONION, QUARTERED

3 MEDIUM CARROTS, 1 QUARTERED AND 2 CUT IN THIN STRIPS

1 BOUQUET GARNI (1 SPRIG PARSLEY, ¼ TEASPOON DRIED OR 1 SPRIG FRESH THYME, AND 1 BAY LEAF, TIED IN A SQUARE OF CHEESECLOTH)

2 MEDIUM TURNIPS, CUT IN THIN STRIPS

2 CELERY STALKS, CUT IN THIN STRIPS

2 LEEKS, WHITE PARTS ONLY, CUT IN THIN STRIPS

4 6-OUNCE FILETS OF WHITING (OR SUBSTITUTE SOLE OR FLOUNDER)

¼ CUP CRÈME FRAÎCHE

SALT AND FRESHLY GROUND BLACK PEPPER

In a large saucepan, brown the fish bones in the butter. Stir in boiling water, wine, shallot, garlic, onion, quartered carrot, and bouquet garni. Bring to a boil, reduce heat, and simmer for 30 minutes. Strain and discard solids.

Steam the julienned vegetables for about 6 minutes, until just tender. Reserve.

Bring the fish stock to a simmer and poach the filets for about 6 minutes. Remove the filets and cover with foil to keep warm. Reduce the stock over high heat to ½ cup. Stir in the crème fraîche and warm over low heat for 2 minutes. Adjust seasonings.

Place the julienned vegetables on a platter. Place the fish on top. Pour the sauce over the fish.

SERVES 4

Cerises à la Savoyarde

[CHERRIES SAVOYARD]

This is a luscious dessert similar to cherries jubilee. The sauce can be made ahead and reheated just before serving.

1½ POUNDS SWEET BING CHERRIES, STEMMED AND PITTED

½ CUP SUGAR

2 CUPS FRUITY WHITE WINE, SUCH AS APREMONT

1 2-INCH STRIP OF ORANGE PEEL

1 CINNAMON STICK

½ VANILLA BEAN

2 TABLESPOONS UNSALTED BUTTER

2 TABLESPOONS KIRSCH

1½ PINTS VANILLA ICE CREAM

Place all ingredients except kirsch and ice cream in a saucepan and bring to a boil. Boil for about 40 to 50 minutes, until liquid is syrupy.

Add the kirsch and carefully light with a match to burn off the alcohol. Spoon the sauce over the ice cream to serve.

SERVES 6 TO 8

. . . .

KIRSCH AND WHITE WINE MAKE THIS CHERRY DESSERT A HEADY FINISH TO A MEAL.

TABLES SET WITH CRISP WHITE LINENS AND ROMANTIC CANDLELIGHT WELCOME EVENING DINERS TO LE VIEUX BISTRO.

LE VIEUX BISTRO

At night, when flickering candlelight fills the small bar of Le Vieux Bistro, with its ancient mottled mirrors and black banquettes, the extraordinary view across the *rue* is obscured. Set among the tacky souvenir emporiums of the Ile-de-la-Cité, this tiny, discreet bistro faces the awesome north wall of Notre Dame Cathedral. For those lunching at Le Vieux Bistro, the great edifice of its neighbor is overwhelmingly "there." But at dinner one is enveloped by the interior's cozy, dim, romantic atmosphere, and the outside world fades into the night.

True to its name, Le Vieux Bistro is more than one hundred years old, while its subcellar, once connected by a stone passageway to the cellars of Notre Dame, dates from the thirteenth century. The restaurant began its life as a *bougnat*—one of the many modest *cafés-charbons* at the turn of the century run by families from the Auvergne, where simple meals as well as coal could be purchased inexpensively. Then, for close to fifty years—from just after World War I through the mid-1960s—it belonged to a woman originally from the north of France remembered only as "Ma Tante," who operated her establishment as a classic bistro known as Chez Ma Tante. Active

. . . .

in the Resistance during World War II, Ma Tante sheltered English aviators in her cellar, while German officers enjoyed themselves upstairs at the zinc bar.

For more than a quarter-century now, Jean Fleury has been the watchful owner of Le Vieux Bistro, managed these days by his brother, the gracious and soft-spoken Fernand, and his nephew, Philippe Rayer. The bar, with its eight small tables where habitués prefer to sit, has been left unchanged from the days of Ma Tante. The back storage area has been transformed into a comfortable, saffron-hued dining room where newcomers and those who didn't reserve their bar table in time take their meals.

Presiding over the kitchen since the late 1970s is Baudouin Verlaeton, a Frenchman of Belgian descent, and a colleague of Fernand Fleury's for more than two decades, since they worked together at the one-star restaurant La Boule d'Or. Monsieur Verlaeton combines classic bistro fare, such as Poireaux Vinaigrette (leeks vinaigrette), beef bourguignon, and crème caramel, with richer, more elaborate dishes such as his Co-

quilles Saint-Jacques au Whisky (scallops with whisky cream sauce), and his Coeur de Filet à la Moëlle en Papillote (a prime, very rare filet of beef cooked in foil with marrow). Everything served from his closet-size kitchen is prepared daily from market-fresh ingredients. There are several clients, presumably without regard for their cholesterol count, who come regularly for these two latter dishes, finishing off their meals with a hearty serving of the house Tarte Tatin (the succulent upside-down, caramelized apple tart, here flambéed with Calvados and served with a pot of crème fraîche).

As old as it is, Le Vieux Bistro is still a discovery. Many Parisians, enchanted by their first dinner at 14 rue du Cloître-Notre-Dame are loathe to share with their acquaintances the address of this little gem set amid the dross of neighborhood tourist traps. Thus, many Paris gourmands have yet to learn about it. And in spite of its location on a street with heavy pedestrian traffic, Monsieur Fleury gets little walk-in trade: "The people off the tour buses come in and are disappointed they can't get a salad and a sandwich, or a plate of cold cuts and a beer. And the more sophisticated diners who are seeking a good restaurant meal look in and don't realize they can get one here. They think we're for salads and sandwiches! Thank goodness eighty-five percent of our customers are regulars. Without habitués, we'd be finished."

The most famous regular was the late president of France, Georges Pompidou. "He came so often," Fleury says, "we were almost like his canteen!" The bistro is still favored by politicians who cross over the bridge from the Hotel de Ville, or City Hall, on the Right Bank, along with a coterie of police commissioners and detectives. Also numbering among the

habitués are chefs from other restaurants who frequent Le Vieux Bistro on their nights off, a felicitous sign. One who appears often on Sunday evenings with his wife and friends is Michel Petit, the acclaimed chef-owner of Benoît, the elegant Right Bank bistro. The restaurant is solidly booked on weekend nights, as well as on occasional holiday eves when other restaurants are closed. In the happy and relaxed atmosphere it is not unusual for guests here to chat from table to table, as if the restaurant were reserved for a private party. One night a year Le Vieux Bistro does indeed become the exclusive haunt of old friends. For many years now, a Scottish family living in Paris has booked the entire bar for a long, festive celebration on New Year's Eve. For those attending this convivial gathering, there is no mistaking the arrival of the New Year; at midnight the whole room reverberates from the pealing bells of Notre Dame.

Rillettes de Saumon

[POACHED SALMON SPREAD]

1 8- TO 12-OUNCE SALMON FILET

1 CUP FISH STOCK (OR ½ CUP CLAM JUICE AND ½ CUP DRY WHITE WINE)

½ CUP (1 STICK) LIGHTLY SALTED BUTTER, AT ROOM TEMPERATURE

1 LARGE SHALLOT, MINCED

½ POUND SMOKED SALMON, CUT IN LONG, VERY THIN STRIPS

PEASANT BREAD OR BAGUETTES

LEMON QUARTERS (OPTIONAL)

In a small fish poacher or medium heavy-bottomed casserole, poach the salmon in the stock for 8 to 10 minutes, depending on thickness. Remove from heat. Lift the salmon from the pan with a long spatula and set aside.

In a heavy-bottomed skillet, melt 1 tablespoon of the butter over medium heat, then add the shallot, cooking just until it is softened and translucent but not browned. Reduce heat to low and add the strips of smoked salmon, stirring to blend with the shallot, then add the poached salmon. With the back of a large wooden spoon, mash the fish and shallot together, working the spoon in long vertical strokes to give the mixture a bit of the classic "stringy" *rillettes* texture. Remove the pan from the heat and blend in the remaining butter with a wooden spoon.

Transfer the salmon *rillettes* to a heavy crock or bowl, cover, and chill for at least 2 hours. Serve by heaping tablespoonfuls with slices of toasted peasant bread or baguettes, and, if desired, quartered lemons.

SERVES 6 TO 8

COQUILLES SAINT-JACQUES IS A TRADITIONAL FAVORITE AT LE VIEUX BISTRO.

. . . .

Coquilles Saint-Jacques au Whisky

[SCALLOPS WITH WHISKY CREAM SAUCE]

1¼ POUNDS SEA SCALLOPS, RINSED

SALT AND FRESHLY GROUND PEPPER

¾ CUP SCOTCH OR IRISH WHISKY

2 CUPS CRÈME FRAÎCHE

1 SPRIG CURLY PARSLEY

Mix the scallops, salt, pepper, and whisky in a skillet and cook over high heat for 2 to 3 minutes, until the scallops are just firm. Strain the liquid from the scallops into a saucepan. Set aside the scallops and cover loosely to keep warm.

Reduce the liquid over high heat by two-thirds, adding any accumulated juices from the scallops. Stir in 1½ cups of the crème fraîche and continue to reduce to ¾ cup. Remove from heat.

Preheat the broiler.

Return the reserved scallops to the pan. Whip the remaining crème fraîche until soft peaks form and fold into the scallops. Place the scallops in a heatproof serving dish and place the dish 2 to 3 inches from the heat for 30 seconds to glaze the surface of the sauce. Decorate the dish with a sprig of curly parsley.

SERVES 4

Poires Belle Hélène

[POACHED PEARS WITH ICE CREAM AND CHOCOLATE SAUCE]

. . . .

PEARS

1½ CUPS SUGAR

2 CUPS WATER

4 RIPE, FIRM PEARS (WITH STEMS), PEELED, LEFT WHOLE, AND CORED AT BOTTOM

2 TABLESPOONS LEMON JUICE

. . . .

CHOCOLATE SAUCE

3½ OUNCES SEMISWEET CHOCOLATE, CHOPPED

½ CUP WATER

. . . .

1 PINT VANILLA ICE CREAM

4 TABLESPOONS TOASTED SLICED ALMONDS

TO PREPARE THE PEARS: Place the sugar and water in a 2-quart saucepan and bring to a boil over moderately high heat. Lower the heat and simmer for 5 minutes. Add the pears and lemon juice and simmer for 15 to 20 minutes, turning pears occasionally, until they are just tender when pierced with the tip of a knife. Let pears cool in the syrup.

TO MAKE THE SAUCE: Place the chocolate and water in a saucepan and stir constantly for about 10 minutes over low heat, until the sauce is smooth and thickened.

To serve, put a drained pear on each dessert plate and place 2 small scoops of ice cream on each side of the pear. Drizzle the pears with chocolate sauce and sprinkle with almonds.

SERVES 4

Poireaux Vinaigrette

[LEEKS VINAIGRETTE]

4½ POUNDS LEEKS, TRIMMED
(ABOUT 6 MEDIUM)

¼ TEASPOON SALT

⅛ TEASPOON FRESHLY GROUND
PEPPER

1 TABLESPOON SHERRY VINEGAR

1 TEASPOON DIJON-STYLE
MUSTARD

4 TABLESPOONS OLIVE OIL

2 TABLESPOONS FINELY
CHOPPED ITALIAN PARSLEY, OR
1 TABLESPOON EACH FINELY
CHOPPED PARSLEY AND TARRAGON

4 PERFECT BOSTON OR ROMAINE
LETTUCE LEAVES

Cut off the outer green leaves of the leeks and trim to pale green just above the whites. Wash the leeks very well in several changes of water, and tie into 2 bunches using kitchen string. Bring a large pot of salted water to the boil and cook the leek bunches for 7 to 9 minutes, until leeks are just tender when pierced with a knife. Let cool in the cooking liquid. Drain well, remove string, and set aside.

. . . .

ONE OF THE SIMPLEST OF LEEK RECIPES
IS POIREAUX VINAIGRETTE.

BEEF MARROW ENRICHES THIS ALREADY SUCCULENT *FILET DE BOEUF* DISH.

. . . .

Place the salt, pepper, vinegar, and the mustard in a small bowl and whisk together. Add the olive oil, whisking until the mixture is well combined. Stir in 1 tablespoon of the chopped parsley or parsley-tarragon mixture. Taste for seasoning, and adjust as necessary.

To serve, arrange lettuce leaves on 4 plates and place the leeks on the leaves. Pour the vinaigrette over the leeks and sprinkle with remaining parsley.

SERVES 4

Coeur de Filet à la Moëlle en Papillotte

[FILET OF BEEF WITH MARROW
EN PAPILLOTTE]

En papillotte describes food cooked in a wrapping of greased paper, wax paper, or foil. This recipe calls for aluminum foil.

12 OUNCES BEEF MARROW
(SEE NOTE)

1½ POUNDS CENTER-CUT FILET
OF BEEF (OFTEN CALLED
CHATEAUBRIAND), AT ROOM
TEMPERATURE

1 TABLESPOON HERBES DE
PROVENCE (SEE NOTE)

SALT AND FRESHLY GROUND
PEPPER

Preheat the oven to 475°F.

Place a 16 × 36-inch piece of aluminum foil on a baking sheet. Cut the marrow into large slices and then place them in the center of the foil.

Rub the meat with the herbs, salt, and pepper and place on top of the marrow. Taking care not to tear the foil, fold the foil over the meat to make a tightly sealed packet. Roast the meat for 15 to 20 minutes.

To serve, open the aluminum foil and place with the meat and marrow on a carving board, keeping any juices in the foil. Slice the meat into 4 servings and place with the marrow on a heated serving platter. Pour any accumulated juices over the meat and marrow and serve.

SERVES 4

NOTE: You will need about 1¼ pounds of bones to yield 12 ounces of marrow.

Herbes de Provence is a mixture of 1 teaspoon dried rosemary, 1 teaspoon dried thyme, and ½ teaspoon each dried basil and marjoram.

Gratin Dauphinois

[OVEN-BAKED POTATOES WITH CHEESE]

1¾ POUNDS POTATOES, PEELED

SALT AND FRESHLY GROUND PEPPER

FRESHLY GRATED NUTMEG

2 CUPS SCALDED MILK

1 LARGE EGG

½ GARLIC CLOVE

3 TABLESPOONS UNSALTED BUTTER

1⅓ CUPS GRATED GRUYÈRE CHEESE

Preheat the oven to 400°F.

Slice the potatoes very thin and place in a large bowl. Toss with salt, pepper, and nutmeg. In a small bowl, gradually beat the hot milk into the egg.

Rub a shallow 2-quart ovenproof baking dish (a gratin or casserole) with the garlic and then with half the butter. Place half of the potato slices in the dish and sprinkle with half of the cheese.

Add the remaining potatoes and pour the milk mixture over the potatoes. Sprinkle with the remaining cheese and dot with the remaining butter.

Bake for 45 to 50 minutes, until well browned and tender. Cover loosely with aluminum foil if the top begins to get too brown.

SERVES 4 TO 6

Tarte Tatin

[UPSIDE-DOWN APPLE TART]

This delicious caramelized apple tart, a bistro favorite, was made famous by two sisters named Tatin who ran a hotel-restaurant in the town of Lamotte-Beuvron early in the 1900s. Serve warm with crème fraîche.

. . . .

PÂTE BRISÉE

¾ CUP ALL-PURPOSE FLOUR

3 TABLESPOONS COLD UNSALTED BUTTER, CUT INTO SMALL PIECES

½ TEASPOON SUGAR

⅛ TEASPOON SALT

. . . .

NEARLY EVERY PARIS BISTRO SERVES A CLASSIC TARTE TATIN, A CARAMELIZED UPSIDE-DOWN APPLE TART.

¼ CUP COLD WATER (OR MORE IF NEEDED)

. . . .

FILLING

8 MEDIUM GOLDEN DELICIOUS APPLES

¾ CUP SUGAR

3 TABLESPOONS UNSALTED BUTTER

2 TABLESPOONS LEMON JUICE

¾ TEASPOON GROUND CINNAMON

TO MAKE THE PÂTE BRISÉE: In a medium bowl, mix the flour, butter, sugar, and salt with your fingers for about 15 seconds. Add the water and form the dough into a ball. On a floured pastry board or other work surface, knead the dough for about 1 minute, until the texture is uniform and the dough has body. Wrap in plastic wrap and chill for 30 minutes.

TO MAKE THE FILLING: Peel the apples, core, and cut each into 8 thick slices. Place the sugar and butter in a 9-inch ovenproof skillet and melt over low heat. Remove from heat. Tightly pack half of the apples into the pan, slightly overlapping the slices. Toss the remaining apples with the lemon juice and add to the pan. Return pan to the heat and simmer about 30 minutes, until the juices are thickened and golden. Remove the pan from the heat and let the apples rest for 5 minutes. Sprinkle with cinnamon.

Meanwhile, preheat the oven to 425°F.

On a lightly floured board, roll out a 9-inch circle of pastry and lay it over the apples. Tuck any rough edges around the apples. Bake for about 20 minutes, until the pastry is golden brown. Cool on a wire rack.

Before serving, preheat the broiler; invert the cake pan onto a heatproof platter; and run the tart 2 to 3 inches under the broiler for about 3 minutes to caramelize the top of the cake.

SERVES 6 TO 8

THE CARVED OAK *COMPTOIR* DOMINATES THE AUTHENTIC NINETEENTH-CENTURY DECOR OF AUX CHARPENTIERS.

AUX CHARPENTIERS

implicité, saveur, et sobriété" is how Pierre Bardèche, proprietor and chef of the classic nineteenth-century Left Bank bistro Aux Charpentiers, succinctly describes his cuisine. In the classic bistro tradition, his approach to cooking is emphatically down to earth. "You can embellish a dish to catch the eye, but it doesn't mean that the taste will be truly satisfying," says this dark-eyed, expressive chef with a southern French heritage. "Food is like a beautiful woman: It is sometimes more dramatic and more appealing when simply and honestly presented."

The food of Aux Charpentiers—bistro classics created with a light touch —is very appealing indeed. Among the regular offerings that change little from season to season is the Caneton Rôti Sauce Olives et Porto (a tender and tasty roast duckling with olives in a savory port-wine sauce); the *raie poché et son beurre noisette aux capres* (poached skate in a sauce of hazelnut butter and capers); and *boudin à l'artisanal, pommes en l'air* (a thick, rustic sausage served with sautéed apples). Some of the regular clients, among them a high proportion of editors and journalists, as well as politicians and *fonction-naires* from the Sénat, make a point to come on a Friday or a Saturday for the acclaimed Aïoli de Morue et Ses Légumes (a colorful platter of

OLD PHOTOGRAPHS RECALL A *TEMPS PERDU* WHEN CARPENTERS FREQUENTED AUX CHARPENTIERS.

. . . .

poached salt cod with bright steamed vegetables, served with a crock of garlic mayonnaise); and the *choux farci campagnard* (a country-style stuffed cabbage with carefully constructed layers of bright green cabbage leaves and meat stuffing, served on Saturdays). This robust fare never leaves patrons feeling uncomfortably full, partly because Chef Bardèche uses butter and flour sparingly. A selection from a well-chosen list of moderately priced wines, among them a variety of Beaujolais—Brouilly, Fleurie, Juliénas—and some light and fruity reds from the Loire—a Bourgueil and an unusual Pinot de Reuilly—accompanies the meal.

A restaurant has stood on the site of Aux Charpentiers since 1856, but it took on its current name only in 1874. Next door to what was the headquarters for the "Compagnons Charpentiers du Devoir de Liberté"—a brotherhood of carpenters with roots in the medieval guild tradition—Aux Charpentiers was for decades the hallowed "local" for the carpenter

members of the "Compagnons." The carpenters' headquarters disappeared from the neighborhood long ago, and the museum of the group's history and works that replaced it has recently moved to new quarters. Now all that remains of the restaurant's association with the carpenters is its name, and a fascinating collection of memorabilia and *objets,* among them several elaborate wooden scale models of towers, turrets, and fantasy dwellings, some long part of the restaurant's decor, some carefully gathered and displayed by Pierre Bardèche after he acquired the restaurant in 1976. The models are in perfect harmony with Aux Charpentiers' authentic late nineteenth- and early twentieth-century decor—wrought-iron window grilles, lace curtains, an antique napkin cabinet, bentwood coatracks, and a carved oak bar, created in 1907, its massive zinc top an exact replica of the one taken away during the Occupation.

The path that led Pierre Bardèche to Aux Charpentiers, an operation he runs with smooth professionalism, was a rocky one. The third generation in Paris of a family originally from Corrèze, a *département* to the west of the Massif Central, Bardèche is also the third—and originally reluctant—generation of Paris restaurateurs. All four of his grandparents migrated up to the capital in the late nineteenth century and established bistros in the north of Paris. "My maternal grandmother, who was a Cordon Bleu chef," Bardèche recalls, "used to prepare one thousand escargots a day before World War I." His parents perpetuated the tradition with their own restaurant, Chez Dupeux, in Montmartre. Even though he knew the restaurant world intimately, and had "always known how to cook," Bardèche decided early in life to seek another career.

"I felt I was a victim of the business," he explains. "The first time I took a vacation with my parents, I was nineteen years old. I had seen the *esclavage* of my parents and grandparents and it wasn't going to be for me." But destiny disagreed and, after frustrating his efforts in other domains during his late teens and early twenties, led him, at the age of twenty-five, to the Royal Printemps, a restaurant on the Boulevard Haussmann. He went on to create and manage the first restaurant established in the Métro, at the Haussmann stop, and later cofounded a Brazilian restaurant, the Via Brazil. Just before buying Aux Charpentiers, he turned down the opportunity to become the European director of operations for McDonald's.

By the time Pierre Bardèche took on Aux Charpentiers, which he runs with the help of his wife, Colette (who also oversees operations at their second establishment, a small fish restaurant called L'Ecaille, down the street), he had come to terms with his calling. "A wonderful old friend, a grand chef

. . . .

AUX CHARPENTIERS OFFERS TWO UNUSUAL WINE-AND-LIQUEUR HOUSE COCKTAILS.

named André Juillot, who's now in his eighties, was responsible for my *révélation de la cuisine*," Bardèche says. "He made me see that to be a chef was a noble profession where one has to be *un ouvrier, un artisan, et un artiste* all at once: a worker for the work of the hands, a craftsman for the work of the head, and an artist for the inspiration of the heart that guides every true chef."

Salade de Choux au Lard

[WHITE CABBAGE SALAD WITH BACON LARDONS]

½ MEDIUM HEAD WHITE CABBAGE

¼ CUP DISTILLED WHITE WINE VINEGAR

SALT AND FRESHLY GROUND PEPPER

½ CUP PEANUT OR VEGETABLE OIL

½ POUND SLAB BACON, CUT INTO SHORT JULIENNE STRIPS

2 TABLESPOONS AGED RED WINE VINEGAR

½ CUP TOASTED CROUTONS (OPTIONAL)

Cut the cabbage half into two pieces, cut out the core, then mince the cabbage roughly to the texture of coleslaw. Place cabbage in a large glass or ceramic salad bowl. In a small saucepan, bring white vinegar to a boil, then remove from heat and pour over cabbage; toss well, season with salt and pepper, and set aside uncovered for 2 hours.

In a medium skillet, heat oil, then add bacon. Cook over medium heat until bacon strips get very brown and crispy, about 15 minutes. Pour bacon and oil over cabbage. Spoon red wine vinegar into skillet and deglaze pan. Pour vinegar over the cabbage mixture and toss well. If using croutons,

sprinkle over top and serve.

If any salad is left over, you can serve it the next day as a *salade tiede*, a lukewarm salad. To recrisp bacon and liquify cold oils, heat remaining salad in a casserole over medium heat for about 5 minutes, tossing frequently. Serve warm.

SERVES 4 TO 6

Caneton Rôti Sauce Olives et Porto

[ROAST DUCKLING WITH OLIVES AND PORT]

At Aux Charpentiers, all the meat is carved from the bone in slices and presented on a platter surrounded by the sauce and accompanied by steamed baby potatoes. You might prefer to cut the duckling into four pieces and surround them with sauce, or to carve the crispy brown bird at the table and serve the sauce on the side. This dish is also excellent served with a combination of long-grain and wild rices.

1 4½-POUND DUCK

SALT AND PEPPER

2 TABLESPOONS OLIVE OIL

1½ CUPS FINELY CHOPPED CARROTS

1½ CUPS FINELY CHOPPED ONIONS

6 GARLIC CLOVES, UNPEELED

½ CUP PEELED, CHOPPED TOMATO

⅛ TEASPOON CINNAMON

¼ TEASPOON ALLSPICE

⅛ TEASPOON CAYENNE

1 TEASPOON SALT

FRESHLY GROUND PEPPER

1 BOUQUET GARNI (1 SPRIG EACH OF PARSLEY AND THYME, 1 BAY LEAF, AND 3 WHOLE CLOVES, TIED IN A SQUARE OF CHEESECLOTH)

½ CUP BRANDY OR COGNAC

1¼ CUPS PORT

1¼ CUPS DRY WHITE WINE

½ CUP PITTED GREEN OLIVES, DRAINED AND RINSED

1 TABLESPOON FINELY CHOPPED PARSLEY

GREEN OLIVES AND PORT DISTINGUISH AUX CHARPENTIERS'S ROAST DUCKLING.

· · · · · · · · · · · ·

Sprinkle the inside of the duck with salt and pepper. Place duck, breast up, in a cold oven. Turn oven to 500°F. Turn duck over, breast to back, several times and cook for 55 minutes. Remove duck from roasting pan and let sit 10 minutes before cutting into serving pieces.

Prepare a sauce by heating the oil in a casserole over medium heat and add the carrots, onions, and garlic. Cover and cook until vegetables are wilted but not browned. Stir in the tomato. Add the cinnamon, allspice, cayenne, salt, pepper, and bouquet garni. Add the brandy and carefully ignite. Add the port and wine and bring to a boil. Lower heat and let sauce reduce for ½ hour. Add ½ cup water and continue to cook for another ½ hour. Strain the sauce into a pan. Add the olives; bring to a boil and reduce until lightly thickened. (This sauce can be prepared an hour or two ahead of time, then reheated before serving). When ready to serve, sprinkle with chopped parsley.

SERVES 4

Gâteau au Chocolat Amer

[BITTERSWEET CHOCOLATE CAKE]

....

GÉNOISE CAKE

5 EGGS

¾ CUP SUGAR

⅔ CUP ALL-PURPOSE FLOUR

½ CUP DUTCH-PROCESSED COCOA

1 TEASPOON BAKING POWDER

3 TABLESPOONS MELTED UNSALTED BUTTER

....

SUGAR SYRUP

⅓ CUP SUGAR

⅓ CUP WATER

2 TABLESPOONS DARK RUM

....

CHOCOLATE MOUSSE FILLING

6 OUNCES SEMISWEET CHOCOLATE

2 OUNCES BITTER CHOCOLATE

5½ TABLESPOONS UNSALTED BUTTER

5 EGGS, SEPARATED

1 CUP HEAVY CREAM

....

GLAZE

4 OUNCES SEMISWEET CHOCOLATE

2 OUNCES BITTER CHOCOLATE

¾ CUP HEAVY CREAM

TO MAKE THE GÉNOISE CAKE: Preheat oven to 350°F. Butter and flour a 9 × 2-inch round baking pan. Place the eggs and the sugar in a double boiler over simmering water and stir until they are warm and sugar is dissolved. Remove from heat. Beat on high speed with electric mixer until pale and thick, about 10 minutes. Sift flour, cocoa, and baking powder together. Fold gradually into egg mixture. Carefully fold in melted butter. Spread evenly in pan and tap pan on hard surface to remove air bubbles. Bake for 30 minutes, until a wooden pick inserted into center of cake comes out clean. Cool on rack for 10 minutes. Unmold cake and cool completely.

TO MAKE THE SUGAR SYRUP: Place the sugar and water in a small saucepan and bring to a boil, stirring occasionally. Cool, and stir in rum.

TO MAKE THE CHOCOLATE MOUSSE FILLING: Place both chocolates and

butter in a double boiler over simmering water and stir until melted. Beat chocolate mixture gradually into the egg yolks. Beat the egg whites until soft peaks form, and carefully fold into chocolate mixture. Whip the cream until soft peaks form; fold into chocolate mixture. Chill mousse at least 1 hour before filling cake.

TO MAKE THE GLAZE: Melt both chocolates and heavy cream together in a saucepan over low heat, stirring often until thick and smooth. The glaze coats the cake best when lukewarm.

To assemble, slice the cake into 3 thin rounds. Brush each round with the sugar syrup. Place the bottom round on a 9-inch round of cardboard and place on a rack. Fill and frost cake layers with mousse. Chill 30 minutes. Place the cake on a cookie sheet. Smooth the top with a spatula dipped in hot water. Pour the warm glaze over the cake, letting it drip over sides. Chill cake until ready to serve.

SERVES 10 TO 12

....

DINERS TRY TO SAVE ROOM FOR CHEF BARDÈCHE'S LUSCIOUS MOUSSE-FILLED CHOCOLATE CAKE, DISPLAYED TEMPTINGLY ON THE BAR.

Terrine de Foie de Porc

[COUNTRY-STYLE PÂTÉ]

1 POUND PORK LIVER

2 POUNDS GROUND PORK

1½ CUPS FINELY CHOPPED ONION

3 GARLIC CLOVES, MINCED

½ CUP FINELY CHOPPED PARSLEY

½ CUP DRY WHITE WINE

¼ TEASPOON CINNAMON

2 TEASPOONS SALT

½ TEASPOON FRESHLY GROUND PEPPER

3 BAY LEAVES

Finely chop the liver and mix together with all remaining ingredi-

SALT COD, A BISTRO STAPLE USUALLY SERVED AS *BRANDADE DE MORUE*, IS GIVEN A
PROVENÇAL SPIN IN AUX CHARPENTIERS'S AÏOLI DE MORUE.

. . . .

ents except bay leaves. Cover and refrigerate for 24 hours.

Preheat oven to 300°F. Place meat mixture in a 9 × 5-inch loaf pan and top with bay leaves. Bake 2 hours. Remove from oven and let cool completely.

Serve in thin slices with grainy mustard and cornichons.

SERVES 8 TO 10

Aïoli de Morue et Ses Légumes

[POACHED SALT COD WITH
VEGETABLES AND
GARLIC MAYONNAISE]

. . . .

GARLIC SAUCE

**3 GARLIC CLOVES,
PEELED**

½ TEASPOON SALT

**½ CUP COOKED WARM MASHED
POTATO**

1 EGG YOLK

¾ CUP OLIVE OIL

. . . .

VEGETABLES

8 SMALL POTATOES, PEELED

**4 MEDIUM CARROTS, PEELED,
CUT IN 2 × ¼-INCH STRIPS**

**2 MEDIUM TURNIPS, PEELED,
CUT IN 2 × ¼-INCH STRIPS**

**4 SMALL LEEKS, TRIMMED, CUT
IN 2 × ¼-INCH STRIPS**

. . . .

**1 POUND SALT COD, SOAKED
OVERNIGHT IN 3 CHANGES OF
COLD WATER**

4 CUPS MILK

1 SPRIG THYME

1 BAY LEAF

6 PEPPERCORNS

1 SPRIG PARSLEY

TO PREPARE THE GARLIC SAUCE:
Using a mortar and pestle, mash the garlic and salt until pureed. Mix in potato and yolk and beat in the olive oil very gradually with a whisk as if making a mayonnaise. Set aside.

TO PREPARE THE VEGETABLES: Steam the small potatoes, covered, for 5 minutes. Add carrots, turnips, and leeks. Cover and steam 8 to 10 minutes, until tender.

Drain the cod from the soaking water; poach over low heat in the milk with the thyme, bay leaf, and peppercorns for 5 minutes.

To serve, place the vegetables and drained cod on a warmed serving platter. Spoon on some of the garlic sauce and garnish with parsley. Pass remaining sauce in a sauceboat.

SERVES 4

Tarte Pralinée aux Poires

[PRALINE AND CREAM PEAR TART]

. . . .

PASTRY

1⅔ CUPS ALL-PURPOSE FLOUR

**5 TABLESPOONS UNSALTED
BUTTER**

½ CUP CONFECTIONERS' SUGAR

2 OUNCES GROUND ALMONDS

YOLK OF 1 LARGE EGG

½ CUP WATER

. . . .

FILLING

2 CUPS HEAVY CREAM

4 LARGE EGGS

¾ CUP SUGAR

**2 OUNCES TOASTED GROUND
ALMONDS OR WALNUTS**

. . . .

**4 PEARS, PEELED, CORED, AND
HALVED**

**¼ CUP MELTED, STRAINED
APRICOT PRESERVES**

Preheat oven to 350°F.
TO MAKE THE PASTRY: Mix all ingredients until smooth. Dough will be sticky. Use well-floured hands to pat dough into a 12-inch tart pan with a removable bottom. Chill.
TO MAKE THE FILLING: Mix together the cream, eggs, sugar, and nuts.

Then place pear halves in tart shell and pour filling over pears. Bake 1 hour, 10 minutes, until filling is set and top is lightly browned. Cool tart completely and brush with apricot preserves.

SERVES 8 TO 10

THE OLD SERVIETTE CABINET OF LA GRILLE ONCE HELD THE LINEN NAPKINS OF REGULAR CUSTOMERS IN ITS MANY DRAWERS.

RESTAURANT DE LA GRILLE

For more than 200 years, the rue du Faubourg-Poissonnière, stretching up toward the northern perimeter of Paris, was the direct route into Les Halles for fishmongers coming from Dieppe to sell their *poissons* at Paris's central market. Along their way, just before crossing what is now the rue La Fayette, the travelers would pass a striking corner cabaret and wine shop, its windows and doors protected by a handsome wrought-iron grille decorated with grape clusters and a head of Bacchus. The Norman fishmongers have disappeared into history along with Les Halles, but what was once the cabaret remains today as the Restaurant de la Grille, a little bistro with a reputation for, appropriately enough, fine fish.

When chef Yves Cullère and his wife, Geneviève, bought the restaurant in 1971, they acquired an antique shell with an interior unchanged since the turn of the century, but furnished with Formica tables and neon lights by the previous occupants. "We owned a historic property that had been unappreciated by our predecessors," says Geneviève. "We wanted to restore its character." Out went the neon and the Formica, and in came the red velvet banquettes, the beveled oval mirrors, the dainty wall lamps, the old brass hatracks,

EIGHTEENTH-CENTURY WROUGHT IRON-
WORK PROTECTS THE WINDOWS OF
LA GRILLE.

. . . .

and Geneviève's collection of antique lace. Smoothed down over the banquettes, draped on the serving tables and curtaining the windows, its pristine whiteness sets off walls painted a deep bordeaux.

The specialty of the house at La Grille is Turbot Grillé avec Beurre Blanc, ranked by many critics among the best in Paris. Yves Cullère is a proud native of Nantes, a coastal city at the southern tip of Brittany where seafood is plentiful and regional fish recipes abound. Yves carried his heritage and the tradition of a fish-dominated cuisine with him to Paris, and developed a limited menu for his bistro that features his special turbot, *brochette de Saint-Jacques au beurre blanc* (a brochette of scallops with beurre blanc).

Despite his affinity for seafood dishes, Yves also offers some good traditional bistro fare, such as *filet de boeuf au poivre vert* (a tender steak filet in a piquant green peppercorn sauce), and a Boeuf Bourguignon à l'Ancienne (old-fashioned beef bourguignon), cooked with mushrooms in a rich, dark sauce prepared with one bot-tle of red Burgundy for each four servings. With the bourguignon comes a delicious Galette de Pommes de Terre (sautéed potato pancake)—crisp, pan-fried potatoes studded with *lardons*. To accompany their meals, most of the regulars—office workers by day and neighbors from the 10th *arrondissement*, some with little dogs in tow, by night—order a red, white, or rosé Ménetou-Salon, the fresh and pleasing, though not well-known, house wine from the Berry region, southwest of Sancerre. For dessert, a course apparently the least inspiring to the chef, La Grille's best offerings are the simplest—pear or strawberry sorbet, a fruit tart, or the Coupe de Curé—a pistachio ice cream sundae.

An intimate family affair, La Grille functions smoothly with only one employee, a young waiter. Yves shops in the morning, then, with Geneviève's help paring and chopping before lunch and dinner, he prepares the day's fare. Completing the family circle are sons Gilles and Alexandre, who wander in and out of the restaurant as if it were—and, of course, it is—their second home; Geneviève's octagenarian second cousin, René, who helps out with odd jobs; a garrulous mynah bird named Sel; and two well-fed boxer dogs, Belle and Sultan. This tight little *ménage* enlivens La Grille Monday through Friday; on weekends, February school vacation, and holidays they decamp to their country house in the Ile-de-France. On one holiday, however, they make an exception. For many years now, on Christmas eve, the Cullères have offered Christmas dinner to the old and lonely residents of their *quartier.* "It's a moment," says Geneviève, "when we can give back just a little bit of the happiness and satisfaction we've been blessed to know during our many years here on the rue du Faubourg-Poissonnière."

Terrine de l'Océan

[SEAFOOD FISH TERRINE]

The recipe for this attractive and unusual seafood terrine is rather involved and time-consuming. On the other hand, it's large enough to serve sixteen people and would be a perfect first course for a buffet dinner party, easy to serve and to eat.

1½ POUNDS PIKE OR SOLE FILET

1 POUND SALMON FILET

1½ POUNDS OCEAN PERCH OR MULLET FILET

1 POUND FISH BONES

1 1-POUND LIVE LOBSTER

4 TABLESPOONS (½ STICK) UNSALTED BUTTER

2 TABLESPOONS COGNAC

1 CUP WATER

2 POUNDS MUSSELS, SCRUBBED AND DEBEARDED

1 POUND LEEKS, WASHED

2 GARLIC CLOVES, FINELY CHOPPED

4 SHALLOTS, FINELY CHOPPED

½ POUND SORREL OR SPINACH, FINELY CHOPPED

1 LARGE BUNCH FRESH TARRAGON, FINELY CHOPPED

1 TEASPOON SALT

¼ TEASPOON FRESHLY GROUND PEPPER

¾ TEASPOON *QUATRE ÉPICES* (⅛ TEASPOON WHITE PEPPER, ¼ TEASPOON GROUND GINGER, ¼ TEASPOON NUTMEG, AND ⅛ TEASPOON GROUND CLOVES)

2 TEASPOONS DIJON-STYLE MUSTARD

3 LARGE EGGS

1 POUND BACON STRIPS, BLANCHED

WHITE OF 1 LARGE EGG

10 OUNCES SEA SCALLOPS, RINSED

1 ENVELOPE UNFLAVORED GELATIN

. . . .

HERB MAYONNAISE

1 CUP MAYONNAISE

1 TABLESPOON CHOPPED CAPERS

1 TABLESPOON MIXED DRIED HERBS (FINES HERBES OR *HERBES DE PROVENCE*) OR 2 TABLESPOONS CHOPPED MIXED FRESH HERBS

Remove any skin from the fish filets and place the skin with the bones in a large pot. Place all of the filets on a baking sheet, separating each kind of fish.

Using a sharp knife, sever the head of the lobster from the body, killing it instantly. Separate the claws from the body. In a saucepan, cook all of the lobster pieces for 3 minutes in 1 tablespoon of the butter over high heat. Add the cognac to the pan and ignite. When the flames die down, remove from the heat and cool. Remove the lobster meat from the tail and claw and set aside with the fish filets. Place the lobster carcass in the large pot with the fish bones.

In a large pot, bring the 1 cup water to a boil; add the mussels and cook over high heat for 5 minutes, until the mussel shells open. Strain the liquid through cheesecloth into the large pot with the fish bones. Remove the mussels from the shells and set them aside with the fish filets.

Chop the whites of the leeks and place the green portions in the pot with the fish bones. In a skillet over medium heat, cook the whites of the leeks with the garlic and shallots in the remaining butter until leeks are softened but not browned, about 5 minutes.

In a food grinder or food processor, grind the pike or sole filets with the lobster meat; place the fish mixture in a bowl. Stir in the cooked vegetables, sorrel, tarragon, salt, pepper, mixed herbs, and mustard. Beat in the eggs and fold in the mussels.

Preheat the oven to 400°F.

Line a 9 × 5-inch loaf pan with bacon slices, placing them from the center of the pan so that they overhang the long edges of the pan. (It is not necessary to line the end of the pan.) Beat the egg white with a fork until it is frothy and brush the bacon with the egg white.

Place one-fourth of the fish mixture on the bottom of the terrine. Add half of the salmon and perch filets. Cover with another one-fourth of the fish mixture. Layer the scallops over the mixture. Add one-fourth more of the fish mixture. Add the remaining salmon and perch filets and finish with a

MADAME CULLÈRE'S ANTIQUE LACES AND LINENS ARE PRESSED AND PRISTINE.

. . . .

layer of the fish mixture. Fold the bacon over the top.

Place the terrine in a bain-marie or a pan filled with hot water to about one-half to two-thirds up the side of the terrine. Place the pans in the preheated oven and bake for 1¼ hours. Remove the terrine and invert onto a rack over a pan to drain. Cool completely and unmold the terrine. Remove the bacon and discard. Return the terrine to the bain-marie or pan and refrigerate.

Add water to cover the fish bones in the large pot and bring to a boil and simmer for 1 hour. Strain and discard solids. Reduce the liquid to 2 cups. Sprinkle in the gelatin and stir until dissolved. Place the pot over a bowl of ice, stirring occasionally until the mixture is syrupy. Pour the liquid into the terrine. Chill overnight.

TO MAKE THE HERB MAYONNAISE: Mix all ingredients.

To serve, dip the terrine into hot water briefly and invert on a serving platter. Slice with a sharp knife. Accompany with the mayonnaise.

. . . .

CHEF YVES CULLÈRE CARRIED THE RECIPE FOR HIS TERRINE DE L'OCÉAN FROM HIS NATIVE NANTES ON THE ATLANTIC COAST TO PARIS.

SERVES 16

Boeuf Bourguignon à l'Ancienne

[OLD-FASHIONED

BEEF BOURGUIGNON]

1½ POUNDS CHUCK ROAST, CUT
INTO LARGE CUBES

2 TABLESPOONS
VEGETABLE OIL

4 TABLESPOONS COGNAC

1 TABLESPOON UNSALTED
BUTTER

1 CUP CHOPPED ONIONS

2 GARLIC CLOVES, CHOPPED

3 MEDIUM CARROTS, CUT INTO
STICKS, 2 × ¼ INCHES

1 TABLESPOON ALL-PURPOSE
FLOUR

4 CUPS DRY RED WINE,
PREFERABLY BURGUNDY

1 CUP WATER

2 TABLESPOONS TOMATO
PASTE

½ POUND SMALL MUSHROOMS

1 BOUQUET GARNI (1 SPRIG
EACH OF PARSLEY AND THYME,
1 BAY LEAF, AND GREENS OF
1 LEEK, TIED IN A SQUARE OF
CHEESECLOTH)

SALT AND FRESHLY GROUND
PEPPER

. . . .

**BOEUF BOURGUIGNON ARRIVES AT THE
TABLE IN INDIVIDUAL CASSEROLES.**

Brown the meat in the oil in a heavy-bottomed casserole. Drain off the fat. Add the cognac and ignite carefully. When flames subside, remove the meat.

Add the butter to the casserole and brown the onions, garlic, and carrots over medium-high heat. Sprinkle in the flour, stirring well. Add the wine and water and stir in the tomato paste, mushrooms, bouquet garni, and the salt and pepper, scraping the bottom and sides of the pan to loosen the browned meat juices.

Return the meat to the casserole, bring to a boil, cover, and lower the heat; simmer for about 2 hours, until the meat is tender. Skim off any surface fat and remove the bouquet garni.

Serve the meat from a heated serving dish.

SERVES 4

Galette de Pommes de Terre

[SAUTÉED POTATO PANCAKE]

¼ POUND SLAB BACON, CUT IN
1 × ¼-INCH STRIPS

½ CUP FINELY SLICED ONION

2 POUNDS POTATOES, PEELED
AND SLICED VERY THIN

4 TABLESPOONS PEANUT OIL

SALT AND FRESHLY GROUND
PEPPER

Sauté the bacon in a 9-inch non-stick skillet until browned and crisp. Add the onion to the pan and cook until soft and translucent but not brown, about 5 minutes. Remove from the pan and set aside. Drain the excess fat from pan.

Toss the potatoes with 2 tablespoons of the oil and the salt and pepper until well coated. Mix in the bacon and onion. Overlap the potato mixture in several layers in

**A POTATO GALETTE COMPLEMENTS MANY
MEAT DISHES.**

. . . .

the skillet. Cover and cook over medium heat for about 20 minutes, shaking pan occasionally, until the pancake bottom is brown.

Slide the potato pancake onto a plate. Add the remaining oil to the skillet and invert the plate over the skillet. Cover the cake and cook for 20 minutes over medium heat. Uncover and cook 10 minutes longer, shaking the pan to loosen the cake.

To serve, slide the potato cake onto a heated serving platter. Cut into wedges.

SERVES 4

Coupe de Curé

[CURATE'S SUNDAE]

An effortless dessert with a dash of style, each Coupe de Curé consists of 3 small scoops of pistachio ice cream generously splashed with green Chartreuse liqueur (an herb liqueur made by Carthusian monks) and topped with a sprinkle of toasted almonds. Serve with light, buttery cookies.

Filet de Hareng Mariné à l'Huile

[MARINATED SMOKED HERRING]

½ POUND SMOKED HERRING

1 CUP MILK

1 CUP WATER

2 MEDIUM ONIONS, THINLY SLICED

2 MEDIUM CARROTS, THINLY SLICED

½ TEASPOON CRUSHED PEPPERCORNS

½ TEASPOON CORIANDER SEEDS, CRUSHED

2 SPRIGS FRESH THYME

2 BAY LEAVES

2 CUPS OLIVE OIL

Soak the herring in the milk and water overnight in the refrigerator. Drain and rinse. In a shallow glass dish, layer the herring between the onions and carrots. Sprinkle with the peppercorns and coriander seeds. Top with the herbs and cover with the olive oil. Marinate overnight.

SERVES 4

. . . .

TURBOT GRILLÉ FOLLOWS THE FISH APPETIZER.

Turbot Grillé avec Beurre Blanc

[GRILLED TURBOT WITH WHITE BUTTER SAUCE]

. . . .

SAUCE

½ CUP WHITE WINE VINEGAR

¼ CUP DRY WHITE WINE

2 SHALLOTS, MINCED

1 TABLESPOON CRÈME FRAÎCHE

7 TABLESPOONS UNSALTED BUTTER, SOFTENED

SALT

. . . .

FISH

1½ POUNDS TURBOT FILET (SEE NOTE)

SALT AND FRESHLY GROUND PEPPER

1 TABLESPOON UNSALTED BUTTER

1 TABLESPOON VEGETABLE OIL

⅓ CUP DRY BREAD CRUMBS

TO MAKE THE SAUCE: Place the vinegar, wine, and shallots in a medium saucepan or the top half of a double boiler over high heat. Reduce the liquid to 1 tablespoon. Place the pan over hot water in another saucepan or a double boiler on low heat. Whisk in the crème fraîche. Whisk in the butter by tablespoons until sauce is creamy. Add salt to taste. Strain into a bowl and set aside. Be careful not to overheat, since the sauce will separate.

Preheat the broiler.

TO PREPARE THE FISH: Place the fish on a baking dish. Season with salt and pepper. Melt the butter with the oil and brush over the fish on both sides. Sprinkle the fish evenly on both sides with the bread crumbs. Place the baking dish 3 to 4 inches from the heat and cook 5 to 8 minutes, depending on the thickness of the fish.

Remove from the broiler and place the fish on a heated serving platter. To simulate grill marks, heat a metal skewer over a flame (protect your fingers) until red hot and press lightly, "branding" the top of the fish. Serve with the prepared sauce.

SERVES 4

NOTE: It is difficult to find whole fish, especially turbot, outside of cities and large towns. A whole large gray sole would be a good substitute. If only filets are available, use either sole or orange roughy.

Tarte aux Fruits Frais

[TART OF FRESH BERRIES]

This dessert consists simply of fresh mixed berries—such as raspberries, strawberries, and blueberries—served in individual prebaked pâte sucrée shells spread with crème fraîche, glazed with strawberry jam thinned with kirsch, and garnished with a sprinkling of toasted shaved almonds.

. . . .

THE ATTRACTIVE TART OF FRESH FRUITS IS SIMPLE TO PREPARE.

TRICOLOR OMELETTE AND CHICKEN LIVER MOUSSE ARE TWO OF MANY APPETIZERS SERVED A L'IMPASSE.

Gâteau de Foie de Volaille
à la Bressane

Coquilles Saint-Jacques
à l'Effilochée d'Endives

Charlotte aux Fraises
. . . .
Omelette Arlequin

Tournedos de Veau à la
Crème de Ciboulette

Fondant Glacé à la Menthe

A L'IMPASSE

[C H E Z   R O B E R T]

a pervasive sense of family imbues this snug little bistro two steps from the handsome place des Vosges with a warmth and an air of well-being that has drawn the neighbors, as well as a number of film personalities, here for three decades. In a sixteenth-century building that was a convent until the French Revolution, the Collard family—Dédée, Robert, and their children Robert *jeune* and Maryse—serves up a rich and soothing *cuisine bourgeoise* that ranges from the classic simplicity of a vegetable potage, to a more involved and unusual Tournedos de Veau à la Crème de Ciboulette (stuffed medallions of veal in a chive cream sauce). House specialties include such traditional bistro favorites as a *poule au pot* (poached stuffed chicken in a pot), *blanquette de veau* (creamy veal stew), *choux farci* (stuffed cabbage), and a *civet de lapin chasseur* (rabbit stew with mushrooms, shallots, and white wine).

"I cook *comme chez moi*," declares Dédée. The fast-talking, gray-haired matriarch has reigned in the kitchen since 1959, when the family took over an uncle's restaurant, Les Récoules, on a small dead-end street—an *impasse*—in the 3rd *arrondissement*. Dédée personifies the rapidly disappearing *cui-* *sine des mères* tradition— the cooking done by robust and unpretentious

A CARICATURE OF DÉDÉE, ROBERT, AND THEIR ESTABLISHMENT CAPTURES THE
LIVELY CAMARADERIE *CHEZ* ROBERT DURING THE LES HALLES YEARS.

. . . .

women who defined bistro cuisine in Lyons and Paris in the first half of the century. She is passionate about her vocation. "I love my work," she says. "I love making good food. I am always tasting, rectifying, until everything is perfect."

Robert *jeune* and Maryse seem to have inherited their mother's talent. These days, to relieve Dédée, who is in her seventh decade, of some of her demanding kitchen responsibilities, son Robert creates all the *entrées*—appetizers—while Maryse acts as *saucier*. Dédée continues to prepare all main courses, aided by Maryse's mate, Hugh Vulcain, the *sous-chef*. Robert *père*, meanwhile, tends the bar and the cash register, making conversation, drinks, and change, and opening the occasional bottle of Champagne to share with patrons and cronies. The other member of the family, the silky, twenty-two-year-old cat, Javel, a living testament to the salubrious effects of bistro cooking, sleeps atop a radiator, or inside an unsuspecting diner's shopping bag.

For many years, from 1914 into the 1960s, the site of A L'Impasse,

situated at the outer limits of the old Les Halles district, was a warehouse and a garage for handcarts, which could be rented by the day by vendors of fruits, flowers, and vegetables. When Dédée's uncle bought the enterprise in 1940, he turned part of the property into a small canteen to feed the vendors quickly and inexpensively. After the Collards arrived to take over this extremely basic bistro in 1959, leaving behind another family café they had operated in Montmartre, they expanded the menu slightly for a clientele that was still composed almost entirely of workers attached to Les Halles. The watershed change for Dédée and Robert came, as it did for so many neighborhood restaurants, in 1969, with the demise of Les Halles. Instead of closing up shop, however, the Collards, then with two teenage children, decided to expand their operation into a more complete bistro. While renovating their property, they chipped off the plaster and discovered underneath stone walls and massive beams dating from the sixteenth century.

A L'Impasse is divided into two

largely unadorned rooms—the long, narrow dining room and the smaller, lace-curtained bar. The Collards foresee a redesigned and expanded interior some time in the future, but for now their two rooms serve two different purposes, menus, and clienteles. Those who want to have a real meal are seated in the main room with its white tablecloths and sconce lighting; installed at tables in the bar are patrons who wish to drink or simply have a quick bite—a sandwich, a slice of tart, or a *steak-frites*. Apart from the old beams and stone walls, there is a distinctive lack of studied decor. "We didn't want anything fancy," says Dédée, "just a bistro that was simple, clean, and good, where those who came would feel at ease." The formula works, and seems to appeal particularly to journalists, many of whom dine daily *chez* Robert, and a handful of international film stars, among them Jeremy Irons, Gérard Dépardieu, Bill Murray, and John Travolta. Also among the habitués are the former members of the Ligue Révolutionnaire, a small, radical political organization that flourished next door in the late 1960s. "They used to come to us as students with very few *sous*," recalls Robert Jr. "Now they come as government deputies and businessmen." Some things change, some things don't, Chez Robert.

Gâteau de Foie
de Volaille à la
Bressane

[CHICKEN LIVER MOUSSE]

. . . .

MOUSSE

10 OUNCES CHICKEN LIVERS
½ CUP ALL-PURPOSE FLOUR
4 LARGE EGGS

YOLKS OF 4 LARGE EGGS

4 TABLESPOONS CRÈME FRAÎCHE

3 CUPS MILK

1 TEASPOON SALT

¼ TEASPOON FRESHLY GROUND PEPPER

⅛ TEASPOON FRESHLY GRATED NUTMEG

1 TABLESPOON MINCED FRESH PARSLEY

1 GARLIC CLOVE, MINCED

CHOPPED PARSLEY, TO GARNISH

. . . .

SAUCE

1 CUP HEAVY CREAM

2 TABLESPOONS MINCED SHALLOTS

1 TABLESPOON TOMATO PASTE

SALT AND PEPPER

JUICE OF ½ LEMON

Preheat the oven to 350°F.

TO MAKE THE MOUSSE: Trim the livers of all fat, connective tissue, and dark spots. Place all of the ingredients in a food processor or blender and puree. Butter a glass or earthenware 9 × 5-inch loaf pan and pour in the puree. Place in a bain-marie or a larger pan filled with very hot water, and bake for about 40 minutes, until firm and a

. . . .

THE CHICKEN LIVER MOUSSE HAS A SILKEN TEXTURE.

knife inserted into center comes out clean. Remove from oven and let cool.

TO MAKE THE SAUCE: In saucepan over medium heat, cook cream with shallots about 25 minutes, until cream is reduced by one-third. Remove from heat and whisk in tomato paste. Season to taste with salt, pepper, and lemon juice.

Unmold mousse onto serving plate and garnish with some of the warm sauce and the chopped parsley. Serve warm or cold, with additional sauce on the side.

SERVES 10 TO 12

Coquilles Saint-Jacques à l'Effilochée d'Endives

[SAUTÉED SEA SCALLOPS WITH CREAMED ENDIVE]

3 TABLESPOONS UNSALTED BUTTER

½ POUND BELGIAN ENDIVE, SHREDDED LENGTHWISE

SALT AND FRESHLY GROUND PEPPER

1 TEASPOON SUGAR

½ CUP HEAVY CREAM

1 POUND SEA SCALLOPS, WASHED AND DRIED

1 TABLESPOON ALL-PURPOSE FLOUR

1 TABLESPOON FINELY CHOPPED FRESH CHERVIL OR PARSLEY

Heat 1 tablespoon of the butter in a small saucepan. Add the endive, salt, pepper, and sugar. Cover and cook over low heat for 15 minutes. Add the cream and correct the seasonings. Simmer uncovered for another 10 minutes. Keep warm.

Sprinkle the scallops with salt and pepper and the flour. Using a nonstick pan, brown the scallops in the remaining butter in 2 batches over high heat for 2 to 3 minutes

SHELLFISH AND ENDIVES OFTEN APPEAR ON BISTRO MENUS.

. . . .

per batch, until cooked through.

To serve, ladle sauce onto a warmed serving platter and arrange scallops over it. Sprinkle with chervil or parsley.

SERVES 4

Charlotte aux Fraises

[STRAWBERRY CHARLOTTE]

2 PINTS STRAWBERRIES, WASHED, HULLED, AND QUARTERED

JUICE OF 1 ORANGE

2 TABLESPOONS KIRSCH

½ CUP MILK

1½ CUPS CRÈME FRAÎCHE

½ CUP CONFECTIONERS' SUGAR

12 LADYFINGERS OR SMALL STRIPS OF SPONGE CAKE (ABOUT 3 × 1 × ½ INCH EACH)

1 CUP RASPBERRIES

¼ CUP GRANULATED SUGAR

6 MINT SPRIGS

Macerate 1 pint of strawberries in the orange juice and kirsch. Whip the milk and crème fraîche with the confectioners' sugar until firm.

Line 6 small dessert bowls (about 6-ounce capacity each) with plastic wrap. Spread about ½ cup of the crème fraîche mixture in the bottom and up the sides of each bowl. Place 2 ladyfingers or pieces of sponge cake in the bottom of each bowl. Divide the macerated strawberries and juices over the ladyfingers. Cover with the remaining ladyfingers and spread with the remaining crème fraîche. Top each bowl with plastic wrap and place a ramekin on top of each to weight the charlotte down. Refrigerate at least 1 hour.

Puree the remaining strawberries with the raspberries and the granulated sugar. Strain to remove the seeds.

To serve, remove the weights and plastic wrap from the tops of the bowls and invert each charlotte onto a chilled dessert plate. Peel off the remaining plastic wrap and spoon strawberry-raspberry puree around each charlotte. Garnish each with a drizzle of puree and a mint sprig.

SERVES 6

....

OMELETTES ARE A TRADITIONAL FRENCH FIRST-COURSE OFFERING; A L'IMPASSE CREATES A BRIGHT, TERRINE-STYLE VARIATION ON THE THEME, SERVED WITH A SALAD AS AN APPETIZER.

Omelette Arlequin

[TRICOLOR OMELETTE]

1¼ POUNDS PLUM TOMATOES, PEELED, SEEDED, AND CHOPPED

3 TABLESPOONS OLIVE OIL

½ TEASPOON DRIED THYME

SALT AND FRESHLY GROUND PEPPER

1½ POUNDS SPINACH

FRESHLY GRATED NUTMEG

9 LARGE EGGS

6 TABLESPOONS HEAVY CREAM

1 CUP GRATED GRUYÈRE CHEESE

Cook the tomatoes in 1½ tablespoons of the olive oil until most of the moisture evaporates. Season with the thyme, salt, and pepper and set aside to cool.

Wash the spinach leaves and cook over medium heat until wilted. Refresh in cold water. Chop finely and squeeze in a kitchen towel. Heat the remaining olive oil in a skillet and stir in spinach. Sauté for several minutes over me-

dium heat. Season with salt, pepper, and nutmeg and set aside to cool.

Preheat the oven to 400°F.

Into each of 3 small bowls, break 3 eggs and add 2 tablespoons of cream. Add salt and pepper to each bowl and beat the mixture in each bowl until well combined. Add the tomatoes to one bowl. Add the spinach to the second bowl. Add the grated cheese to the third bowl.

Oil an 8 × 4½-inch loaf pan. Place the tomato mixture in the bottom of the pan. Place the pan in a larger pan half-filled with hot water. Bake in the oven for about 15 minutes, until the tomato layer is firm. Pour on the spinach mixture and bake another 15 minutes. Add the cheese mixture and bake about 25 minutes, until the omelette is puffed and lightly golden. Remove from the oven and the outer pan of water. Run a knife around the edges of the pan to loosen the omelette and invert it onto a plate. Reinvert the omelette onto a serving platter. Serve hot or at room temperature with a green salad tossed with olives and a bit of olive oil.

SERVES 6 TO 8

Tournedos de Veau à la Crème de Ciboulette

[STUFFED MEDALLIONS OF VEAL IN CHIVE CREAM SAUCE]

....

VEAL

1 2-POUND BONELESS VEAL TENDERLOIN (SEE NOTE)

SALT AND FRESHLY GROUND PEPPER

2 TABLESPOONS UNSALTED BUTTER

8 FRESH MUSHROOMS, FINELY CHOPPED

STUFFED MEDALLIONS OF VEAL GO WELL WITH A SIDE DISH OF PARSLEYED NOODLES.

. . . .

2 MEDIUM CARROTS, FINELY CHOPPED

¼ STALK CELERY, FINELY CHOPPED

½ TEASPOON DRIED THYME

1 TABLESPOON VEGETABLE OIL

. . . .

CHIVE SAUCE

½ CUP WHITE WINE

5 SHALLOTS, MINCED

1¼ CUPS HEAVY CREAM

½ BEEF BOUILLON CUBE

1 TABLESPOON LEMON JUICE

1 SMALL BUNCH SPINACH (ABOUT 2 OUNCES), WASHED

2 BUNCHES CHIVES (ABOUT 1½ OUNCES)

4 TABLESPOONS (½ STICK) UNSALTED BUTTER, MELTED

TO PREPARE THE VEAL: Trim any fat from the veal and butterfly the meat by making a lengthwise cut almost through it. Spread the tenderloin open and sprinkle with salt and pepper. Melt the butter in a small saucepan and add the mushrooms, carrots, celery, and thyme. Sauté over medium-low heat until the vegetables soften, about 10 minutes. Season with salt and pepper and set aside to cool.

Spoon the vegetable mixture onto the veal, close up the veal, and tie into a cylinder with kitchen string. Wipe the veal dry and brown in the oil on all sides in a heavy-bottomed skillet over medium-high heat. Lower the heat and continue cooking, turning often, for about 10 minutes longer.

TO PREPARE THE CHIVE SAUCE: Meanwhile, place the wine and shallots in a nonreactive saucepan and reduce the liquid over high heat to 1 tablespoon. In a small skillet reduce the cream, bouillon cube, and lemon juice by half. Place the spinach, chives, and melted butter in a food processor or blender and puree. Add the wine and shallots and the cream mixture; process until smooth. Set aside.

Let the veal rest 5 minutes covered loosely with foil. Drain the oil from the skillet and pour in the chive sauce and heat, scraping the sides of the pan with a spoon. Remove the string from the veal and slice in ½-inch slices across the grain. Place on a warmed serving platter and surround with the chive sauce.

SERVES 4

NOTE: Boneless pork tenderloin may be used as a economical substitute for the veal.

Fondant Glacé à la Menthe

[SOFT MINT ICE CREAM WITH CHOCOLATE SAUCE]

The ice cream in this dazzling and delicious dessert is soft and very creamy. It can be kept frozen for at least one week. The sauce can also be made ahead and rewarmed.

1 CUP WATER

1⅓ CUPS SUGAR

YOLKS OF 8 LARGE EGGS

1⅔ CUPS HEAVY CREAM

6 TABLESPOONS MINT SYRUP (SEE NOTE)

6 TABLESPOONS PEPPERMINT SCHNAPPS

4 OUNCES SEMISWEET CHOCOLATE

Bring ⅔ cup of the water and the sugar to a boil. Using a candy thermometer, cook the sugar syrup until it reaches 238°F., or the soft-ball stage.

Beat the egg yolks briefly in an electric mixer on low speed and then very gradually add the sugar syrup to the yolks. Increase to high speed and beat the yolks until cool, about 10 minutes. The mixture will be pale and thick.

Whip the cream until firm and fold in the mint syrup and the schnapps. Fold the cream mixture into the egg yolks and pour into a 9 × 5-inch loaf pan lined with plastic wrap. Cover with more plastic and freeze overnight.

In a heavy-bottomed saucepan, melt the chocolate in remaining ⅓ cup water, stirring often, over low heat until very smooth. Let cool slightly.

To serve, remove the plastic wrap and invert the loaf pan onto a chilled serving platter. Pour a little mint syrup over the ice cream and spoon the warm chocolate sauce around the ice cream.

SERVES 8 TO 10

NOTE: Mint syrup is available from Balducci's (see the Directory for the address).

A NEIGHBOR PAUSES UNDER THE ARCADE OUTSIDE LA FONTAINE DE MARS.

Champignons à la Grecque

Fricassée de Canard aux
Haricots Blancs

Tartelettes aux Poires

············

Oeufs Durs Mayonnaise

Daurade à la Provençale

Gâteau de Semoule

La Fontaine de Mars

The rue Saint-Dominique is a long, narrow street of shops that winds its way through the 7th *arrondissement* in the shadow of the Eiffel Tower. Although the commercial character of the street—which is lined with boutiques, bakeries, butchers, charcuteries, and flower shops—has remained constant for more than 150 years, the businesses themselves have turned over many times, with clothing boutiques, towel shops, and shoe stores gaining on the aging shoemakers, ironmongers, and bric-à-brac shops.

Although turnover is the rule on the rue Saint-Dominique, there are several stubborn exceptions, among them the prime corner property at number 129, the venerable Fontaine de Mars. Since 1900 an inviting golden glow emanating from the windows of this old bistro has warmed the blue-hued Paris dusk, causing many passersby to pause, peer in, and enter.

For nearly a century, the Fontaine de Mars, operated for the last twenty-five years by chef Paul Launay and his wife, An-drée, has been serving simple, substantial fare to the neighborhood ha-bitués and the occasional visitor wandering over from the Eiffel Tower. The name and the owners have changed several times in the last 100 years, and the decor was

THE FONTAINE DE MARS MENU IS STILL
MIMEOGRAPHED EVERY DAY.

. . . .

refurbished once, in 1933, but the space and its function have remained essentially unchanged since the Belle Epoque. In the early days it was a *café-charbon*—a bar where neighbors would come to buy their coal and firewood, have a glass or two of the house red, or a nip of Calvados, and perhaps grab a quick *casse-croûte* (snack). The bistro's name derives from the fountain topped by a statue of the god Mars that dominates a tiny plaza facing the restaurant. "The fountain was constructed in 1806," relates Madame Launay, "in what was then a courtyard surrounded by a military hospital. Mars, the god of war, was chosen to symbolize the glories of military endeavor." Almost twenty feet high, the fountain houses the original pump from 1806, although it is no longer functional.

Since they acquired the Fontaine de Mars in 1966, after coming north from their native Cahors in southwest France, the Launays have maintained their bistro's traditional menu and immutable decor. The essential zinc bar, here located in the back of the restau-

rant near the kitchen, is backed by an intricate oak cupboard of narrow shelves and cubbyholes built by a neighborhood carpenter in 1930. The tables are of thick oak with marble inlays, but are usually out of sight under the bistro's pink-and-white-checked table linen. In a corner near the curtained glass doors, next to an ancient bentwood coatrack, sits a rare piece of furniture that was once a fixture in any thriving bistro—a *meuble à serviettes*—a napkin cabinet set with tiny numbered drawers, this one of oak and rose marble, with enamel numbers on each drawer. Each regular customer was assigned a number corresponding to a numbered drawer. The diner's napkin, neatly rolled, awaited him each night in his drawer and was laundered each week. This quaint practice was eventually prohibited by the hygiene laws of 1948.

Paul and Andrée Launay run a classic operation. He is the exclusive chef, rarely seen in the dining room; she functions as hostess, maître d', captain, and cashier. She also does the morning marketing. He is Monsieur Intérieur, she is Madame Extérieure. The food, honest *cuisine familiale*, features a Fricassée de Canard aux Haricots Blancs (duck fricassee with white beans), inspired by the cuisine of the Southwest, Daurade à la Provençale (porgy Provençal style), and *pintadeau au chou* (guinea hen with cabbage) among their daily specials. The house wine is a rich and rustic Cahors. The old-style menu is rewritten daily. Each morning, after visiting the market, Madame Launay inscribes the day's fare on a master sheet, which is then mimeographed in violet ink on heavy stock under the restaurant's logo.

The dinner hour *chez* Launay is early and short compared to other Paris restaurants—7:00 P.M. to 9:30 P.M. The clientele consists mainly

of neighborhood regulars, as well as a smattering of tourists lingering in the area after paying homage to the Eiffel Tower. Here, as in other bistros, it is not unusual to see lone diners enjoying dinner for one. For them, the restaurant supplies a rackful of newspapers and magazines. At closing time, friends and neighbors occasionally drop in for some local gossip at the old zinc.

La Fontaine de Mars is the kind of simple bistro that is slowly disappearing from the face of Paris, replaced by more fashionable, more profitable enterprises. With both Launays well into middle age, and almost thirty years of hard work behind them, the days of this old gem, a holdout for so long, may be numbered.

Champignons à la Grecque

[MUSHROOMS À LA GRECQUE]

1½ CUPS FINELY CHOPPED
ONIONS

¼ CUP OLIVE OIL

1 POUND MUSHROOMS,
QUARTERED

¼ CUP LEMON JUICE

2 MEDIUM TOMATOES, CORED
AND QUARTERED

SALT AND FRESHLY GROUND
PEPPER

PINCH CAYENNE

A FEW CORIANDER SEEDS

1 CUP DRY WHITE WINE

1 TABLESPOON FINELY CHOPPED
ITALIAN PARSLEY

In a large skillet, sauté the onions in the olive oil until wilted but not browned, about 5 minutes. Toss the mushrooms with the lemon juice, then add to the onions and sauté 3 minutes longer. Add all of the remaining ingredients except the parsley, bring to a simmer, cover, and let simmer over low heat about 20 minutes.

APPETIZERS AT THE FONTAINE DE MARS ARE SIMPLE AND CLASSIC; HERE ARE THE
OEUFS MAYO AND THE CHAMPIGNONS À LA GRECQUE.

. . . .

Let cool completely. Sprinkle with the parsley. If made in advance and refrigerated, bring to room temperature before serving.

SERVES 4

Fricassée de Canard aux Haricots Blancs

[DUCK FRICASSEE WITH WHITE BEANS]

. . . .

DUCK

2 4-POUND DUCKS

3 TABLESPOONS OLIVE OIL

4 TABLESPOONS ALL-PURPOSE FLOUR

1 CUP CHOPPED ONION

3 MEDIUM CARROTS, THINLY SLICED

1 BOUQUET GARNI (1 SPRIG EACH THYME AND PARSLEY, 1 BAY LEAF, TIED IN A SQUARE OF CHEESECLOTH)

1 CUP DRY WHITE WINE

SALT AND FRESHLY GROUND PEPPER

. . . .

HARICOTS BLANCS

1½ CUPS DRIED WHITE BEANS, SOAKED IN WATER OVERNIGHT

2 ¼-INCH SLICES SALT PORK RIND, BLANCHED AND COARSELY CHOPPED

1 SPRIG FRESH THYME, OR ½ TEASPOON DRIED

TO PREPARE THE DUCK: Cut the ducks into serving pieces—breasts, legs, thighs, wings—removing as much fat as possible. Prick the skin with a fork. Dry with paper towels.

In a large skillet over medium-high heat, brown the duck in olive oil, turning until the pieces are golden brown on all sides. Remove the duck, drain all but 3 table-spoons of oil from the pan, and return the duck to the pan. Sprinkle with the flour, stirring until all pieces are well coated.

Add the onion, carrots, bouquet garni, wine, and salt and pepper to taste. Bring to a boil, then cover and reduce heat to medium-low. Simmer for 1 hour and 15 minutes. TO PREPARE THE BEANS: Drain the water from the beans and discard. In a saucepan, combine beans, 2 cups of clean water, the pork rind, and the thyme. Bring to a boil, then cover and let simmer over medium heat for 1 hour. Drain just before adding to the duck.

Remove the duck and skim any surface fat from the sauce. Return the duck to the pan, add the Hari-cots Blancs, correct the seasonings, and let cook about 10 minutes, until hot.

SERVES 4 TO 6

Tartelettes aux Poires

[INDIVIDUAL PEAR TARTS]

PÂTE BRISÉE (SEE PAGE 37)

. . . .

CRÈME PATISSIÈRE

1 CUP MILK

YOLK OF 3 LARGE EGGS

3 TABLESPOONS GRANULATED SUGAR

1½ TABLESPOONS ALL-PURPOSE FLOUR

½ TEASPOON VANILLA EXTRACT

. . . .

POACHED PEARS

2 RIPE, FIRM PEARS

¼ CUP GRANULATED SUGAR

1 CUP WATER

JUICE OF ½ LEMON

CONFECTIONERS' SUGAR

Prepare Pâte Brisée.

Preheat the oven to 400°F.

Divide the chilled dough into fourths. With a floured rolling pin on a floured work surface, roll out each piece to fit 4 greased tartelette molds. Press the dough into the molds. Prick the bottom of the shells with a fork, then crimp the edges to make a tiny rim. Line the shells with foil and fill with pastry pellets. Bake for 10 minutes. Remove the paper and weights and bake 7 to 8 minutes longer, until golden brown. Then make the Crème Patissière on page 62.

CAHORS, A LUSTY WINE FROM FRANCE'S SOUTHWEST, ACCOMPANIES A SALAD APPETIZER AND DUCK FRICASSEE WITH WHITE BEANS.

TO MAKE THE CRÈME PATISSIÈRE: In a medium saucepan over medium heat, scald the milk. Remove from heat. In a small bowl, whisk together the yolks and sugar until thickened. Whisk in the flour until blended. Gradually whisk the hot milk into the egg mixture, until the mixture is smooth. Pour the mixture into a saucepan and set over medium heat. Bring to a boil, whisking constantly. Lower the heat to medium-low and simmer, still whisking, for 2 minutes. Remove from heat, stir in the vanilla, cover with plastic wrap, and let the crème cool.

TO MAKE THE POACHED PEARS: Peel the pears, slice in half lengthwise, and remove the cores. Place in a saucepan with the granulated sugar, water, and lemon juice and bring to a boil over high heat. Lower the heat to medium, cover, and cook for 15 minutes. Remove from heat and let cool in the syrup.

Just before serving, fill each pastry shell with the pastry crème. Cut the pear halves into ¼-inch slices, being careful to preserve the form of the pear. Carefully lift each pear half with a spatula and slide it onto a shell. Sprinkle pears with confectioners' sugar and place 2 to 3 inches under broiler to caramelize.

SERVES 4

Oeufs Durs Mayonnaise

[HARD-COOKED EGGS WITH MAYONNAISE]

6 LARGE HARD-COOKED EGGS, COOLED

6 CRISP LARGE BOSTON OR BIBB LETTUCE LEAVES

2 TABLESPOONS MINCED FRESH PARSLEY, FOR GARNISH

· · · · · · · · · ·

MAYONNAISE

YOLK OF 1 LARGE EGG (SEE NOTE)

1 TEASPOON DIJON-STYLE MUSTARD

2 TEASPOONS WINE VINEGAR

SALT AND FRESHLY GROUND PEPPER

1½ CUPS PEANUT, CORN, OR SUNFLOWER OIL

· · · · · · · · · · · ·

WHILE MANY BISTROS STILL COVER THEIR TABLES WITH PAPER, CHERRY-PINK— CHECKED LINENS CREATE A REFINED BACKDROP FOR THIS TARTELETTE.

Peel the hard-cooked eggs, rinse, and pat dry. Set aside.

TO MAKE THE MAYONNAISE: In a deep bowl, whisk together the egg yolk, mustard, 1 teaspoon of the vinegar, and salt and pepper. When blended, slowly drizzle in the oil, whisking constantly so that the mayonnaise does not curdle. When the mixture is thick and creamy, add salt, pepper, and vinegar to taste.

Cover 6 salad plates with the lettuce leaves. Cut each egg in half vertically and arrange 2 halves on each plate. Cover the eggs with the mayonnaise. Garnish with parsley.

SERVES 6

NOTE: If you are concerned about raw eggs, substitute 1½ cups commercial mayonnaise for the egg yolk, oil, and vinegar, and add the mustard, pepper, and a bit of lemon juice to perk up the flavor.

Daurade à la Provençale

[PORGY PROVENÇAL STYLE]

1 CUP THINLY SLICED ONION

2 TABLESPOONS OLIVE OIL

2 RIPE TOMATOES, SLICED

2 8-OUNCE FILETS OF PORGY, RED SNAPPER, GROUPER, OR ORANGE ROUGHY (SEE NOTE)

SALT AND FRESHLY GROUND PEPPER

1 BOUQUET GARNI (1 SPRIG EACH THYME AND PARSLEY, AND 1 BAY LEAF, TIED IN A SQUARE OF CHEESECLOTH)

PINCH SAFFRON

1 CUP DRY WHITE WINE

1 TABLESPOON TOMATO PASTE

1 TABLESPOON CHOPPED FRESH PARSLEY

Preheat the oven to 350°F.

Sauté the onion in the oil very slowly until soft, not browned, 7 to 10 minutes. Toss in the tomatoes and cook 2 more minutes. Remove pan from heat and set aside.

Place the fish in a shallow baking dish and sprinkle with salt and

PAUL LAUNAY TAKES INSPIRATION FROM
THE MIDI IN HIS BAKED *DAURADE*.

· · · · · · · · · · · ·

pepper. Place bouquet garni between filets. Dissolve the saffron in the wine, and then stir in the tomato paste.

Strew vegetables over and around fish. Pour the wine mixture over the fish and vegetables, and bake 30 minutes. Sprinkle with parsley before serving. Serve with white rice.

SERVES 2

NOTE: Daurade is a Mediterranean fish unavailable in the United States. These fish are good substitutes.

Gâteau de Semoule

[SEMOLINA CAKE
WITH CRÈME ANGLAISE]

· · · · · · · · · · ·

CAKE

1 QUART MILK
1 VANILLA BEAN, OR 1 TEASPOON
VANILLA EXTRACT
6 TABLESPOONS SUGAR
1 CUP SEMOLINA OR COUSCOUS
½ CUP SUGAR AND

1 TABLESPOON WATER, FOR
CARAMELIZING MOLD
1 (7-OUNCE) PACKAGE DICED
MIXED DRIED FRUITS (1¼ CUPS)
YOLKS OF 3 LARGE EGGS

· · · · · · · · · ·

CRÈME ANGLAISE

YOLKS OF 6 LARGE EGGS
⅓ CUP SUGAR
2 CUPS MILK
1 TEASPOON VANILLA EXTRACT

Preheat the oven to 350°F.

TO MAKE THE CAKE: In a saucepan, combine the milk, vanilla bean, and the 6 tablespoons of sugar. Bring the mixture to a boil over medium-high heat. Remove the vanilla bean. Sprinkle in the semolina, stirring constantly. Lower the heat to medium-low and cook slowly, stirring occasionally until the mixture is very thick, about 5 minutes. Remove from heat and let cool slightly. (If not using a vanilla bean, stir in the vanilla extract.)

Heat the sugar-water mixture in a small, heavy-bottomed saucepan over medium heat until the sugar caramelizes to an amber color. Pour immediately into a small ovenproof Kügelhopf mold, or small soufflé dish, coating the interior completely.

Stir the mixed dried fruit and yolks into the semolina mixture, then pour into the caramelized mold. Set mold into a large pan of water. Put in the preheated oven and cook 30 to 35 minutes, until the pudding shrinks slightly from the sides of the mold. Cool on a rack. Invert on a serving plate and set aside.

TO MAKE THE CRÈME ANGLAISE: In a saucepan, whisk together the yolks and the sugar. In another saucepan, heat the milk and the vanilla until hot but not boiling. Pour the hot milk into the yolk mixture, stirring constantly with a spoon. Set over medium heat and stir until the sauce coats the back of the spoon. Do not let the sauce come to a boil or it will curdle. Remove from the heat and place plastic wrap directly on the surface to prevent a skin from forming. Let cool. Remove the plastic wrap, and pass the Crème Anglaise separately with the semolina cake.

SERVES 4 TO 6

· · · · · · · · · · · ·

A KIND OF FRUIT CAKE, THE GATEAU DE SEMOULE MAY ALSO BE MADE
WITH COUSCOUS.

DE LUXE

Benoît

. . . .

D'Chez Eux

. . . .

Chez Georges

THE ELEGANT DINING ROOM AND REFINED CUISINE OF BENOÎT ATTRACT A HOST OF FASHIONABLE CLIENTS.

BENÔIT

Behind the gilded, wrought-iron door of Benôit lies a bistro so refined, so stylish, and so successful that Michel Petit, the chef and owner, has nearly raised his restaurant out of the simple bistro category. Yet in terms of its menu, its tradition, its ambiance, and its high-spirited waiters, Benôit still merits the classification of bistro, albeit a luxurious one. It is, in the words of the Paris restaurant critic Claude Lebey, "the Rolls-Royce of Paris bistros."

Petit, a tall, imposing Norman, has brilliantly perpetuated the establishment founded by his grandfather, Benôit Matray, in 1912. The long tradition of supreme quality and contagious conviviality that defines Benôit today began as soon as Matray opened his door a block away from the Hôtel de Ville, the Paris city hall, and four blocks from Les Halles.

Benôit's story begins in 1904, when Benôit Matray, an ambitious eighteen-year-old butcher, came to Paris from his native Lyon to visit his Uncle Martin, who had a small restau-  rant, A La Ville de Caen, in the Halles district. So impressed was the young Benôit by Uncle Martin's operation that he decid- ed, soon after his arrival in Paris, to abandon his vocation as butcher and pursue his dream of own- ing his own restaurant. For the next seven years

BENOÎT'S GILDED DOOR OPENS ONTO THE
RUE SAINT-MARTIN.

. . . .

THE NOSTALGIC MENU ANNOUNCES
SPECIALITÉS DU JOUR.

. . . .

he worked long hours as an employee of his uncle's, as well as of other restaurateurs, saving every *sou*. In 1912 he proudly announced to his uncle that he was about to open his own restaurant, Chez Benoît, just a few minutes' walk from A La Ville de Caen at 20 rue Saint-Martin. *"Tu as fais une connerie—you've made a stupid mistake,"* replied Uncle Martin. "Les Halles won't last forever."

At the outbreak of *la guerre de quatorze* (World War I), Benoît, along with all his able-bodied compatriots, went off to serve his country. He returned to Paris in 1917, seriously wounded, deeply troubled, but ready, nevertheless, to re-establish himself at the helm of his namesake. Chez Benoît flourished *entre deux guerres*. A bon vivant, and a grand gourmand of great charisma who weighed over 300 pounds in his later years, Benoît Matray was as much of an attraction as the hearty, simple home-style cooking he offered. "Everybody loved him," remembers Michel Petit. "He was *un personnage.*" In the 1932 edition of a

restaurant guide sponsored by Escoffier, the entry for Chez Benoît notes that "Mr. Matray will receive you like a friend afflicted with a beautiful wife." Journalists, politicians, tradesmen from Les Halles, and a number of celebrated show people formed a nucleus of faithful clients. He never kept a *livre d'or* [a guest book], but if he had, prominent among the signers would have been Edith Piaf, who always arrived, notes Chef Petit, looking like *"une vestiaire*—a hat-check lady," and especially Orson Welles. "These two huge men," Chef Petit says, "one was as big as the other, and they adored each other!"

Benoît himself was not a chef; the food *chez* Benoît was prepared by a series of *mères*, the anonymous, working-class women who toiled in the kitchens of bistros of the era. One of these women, a huge, mustachioed figure named Marie, worked with Benoît for twenty-five years, from 1925 to 1950, and it was her cooking that established culinary tradition at the restaurant. "Bistro cooking in those days," says Michel Petit, "was somewhat different than it is today. There were more dishes using *abats*—offal, or variety meats, like kidneys, sweetbreads, hearts, intestines—the leftovers of Les Halles. And meals were generally less sweet—less sugar in the preparation of food and many fewer desserts. Most diners finished their meals with cheese as an excuse to order another bottle of wine. The meal was very simple— a small appetizer, a copious main course, and then the cheese. These diners would have found the concept of a *menu dégustation*, with all the 'tasting' courses, ridiculous."

Michel Petit joined the Benoît enterprise in 1959, when his grandfather was seventy-three and, after almost fifty years in the business, "had had enough." After his military service and then several years

as a chef on the great old French Line ship, the *Liberté*, Petit had returned to Normandy to run his family's inn in the town of Gaillon. Then the call came from his grandfather to take over the day-to-day operation of Benoît. "From 1959 to 1961 I had two businesses under my arm," Petit relates. "I was still trying to keep the inn going while I was running Benoît. Finally I had to make a choice. I had to follow either my heart or my head. Not without *chagrin*, I chose my head."

Michel Petit's cuisine is bistro fare raised to the sublime. He makes the traditional pot-au-feu, but it is served cold as an intensely flavored salad going under the name Compotiers de Boeuf à la Parisienne, and is accompanied by crunchy cornichons, pickled onions, and white crocks of potato salad and *céleri rémoulade*; he makes a *blanquette de veau* from a whole shank of the finest veal; and his roast farm chicken cooks in a lacy crust of coarse sea salt.

The superb fare *chez* Benoît is enhanced by a Vieux Paris decor of period etched glass, cherry-red velour banquettes, bentwood coat-racks, polished brass hat racks, and *faux-marbre* walls. Greeting guests as they enter is a huge spray of fresh flowers, the colors changing with the seasons, on a corner of the mirrored oak bar. For lone diners, daily papers—*Le Monde, Le Figaro*—hang from brass rails running above the banquettes. Guests sit in either the front room—the Benoît restaurant in the early years—or the newer back room, created from a neighboring boutique. On crowded nights tables are also set up in the bar, a prime spot for viewing Benoît's sophisticated clientele but somewhat breezy for dinner. An upstairs room for private parties, recently renovated, is "less bistro, more bourgeois," as chef Petit describes it. Resplendent in red, gold, and etched glass, the *salon privé* is a room in a Napoleon III mood.

With his great success that includes a *Michelin* star, Michel Petit is occasionally asked why he chooses to continue operating a comparatively small, bistro-style operation rather than expand into the domain of haute cuisine, or perhaps, like some of his *confrères*, inaugurate a "Benoît II" in another part of town to accommodate a clientele that could fill his restaurant twice-over every night. A reflective and articulate man, Michel Petit considers the question carefully before replying. "There is great wisdom in knowing how to limit one's ambition, in not being too gourmand in one's approach to life," says this philosopher-chef.

BENOÎT'S *CHOUQUETTES* ARE PERFECT
SERVED BEFORE DINNER.
. . . .

"Choquettes" au Fromage

[CHEESE PUFFS]

After they are seated, diners *chez* Benoît are offered a small plateful of these delicious, airy cheese puffs to quell their hunger pangs as they peruse the menu.

3 TABLESPOONS UNSALTED
BUTTER, CUT INTO BITS

½ CUP WATER

PINCH SALT

¾ CUP SIFTED ALL-PURPOSE
FLOUR

3 LARGE EGGS
¾ CUP SHREDDED GRUYÈRE
CHEESE

In a small saucepan, combine the butter, water, and salt. Bring to a boil over high heat, then remove from the heat and stir in the flour with a wooden spoon. Return to the heat and beat until the mixture becomes very thick and begins to film the bottom of the saucepan.

Preheat the oven to 400°F.

Butter and flour a baking sheet. Add the eggs to the mixture one by one, whipping vigorously with a whisk. The dough should have the consistency of a thick mayonnaise. Stir in the cheese.

Drop walnut-size spoonfuls of dough onto the baking sheet, evenly spaced. Bake 20 to 25 minutes. The puffs will swell to nearly triple in size and become golden.

Turn off the oven and let the puffs cool to lukewarm with the oven door open.

Serve the *"choquettes"* lukewarm with an apéritif or accompanied by a salad as an appetizer.

SERVES 16 TO 18

. . . .

MICHEL PETIT TAKES THE LUNCHTIME ORDERS OF TWO HABITUÉS IN THE FRONT
DINING ROOM, THE RESTAURANT'S OLDEST SECTION, DATING FROM 1912.

Filet de Saumon Fumé Mariné

[HERB-MARINATED SMOKED SALMON]

- 1 32-OUNCE SMOKED SALMON, IN ONE PIECE
- 4 MEDIUM CARROTS, SLICED INTO THIN ROUNDS
- 4 SHALLOTS, FINELY CHOPPED
- 2 LARGE ONIONS, SLICED THIN
- 1 TABLESPOON COARSELY GROUND PEPPER
- 2 BAY LEAVES
- 1 SPRIG THYME
- 1 CUP SUNFLOWER OIL

Cut the salmon into thin slices and place in a shallow glass or earthenware dish. Combine the carrots, shallots, onions, pepper, and herbs; spread the mixture evenly over the salmon and cover with the oil. Cover and marinate overnight.

Serve with cold steamed potatoes. For an impressive garnish, sprinkle with snipped chives and salmon caviar.

SERVES 12

. . . .

MARINATED SMOKED SALMON IS SERVED ON NAPOLEON III—STYLE PORCELAIN.

Boeuf à la Mode

[BRAISED BEEF AND CARROTS]

. . . .

BEEF

- 1 5- TO 5½-POUND WELL-MARBLED BONELESS RUMP OR CHUCK ROAST
- 2 TABLESPOONS OLIVE OIL
- 1½ POUNDS CARROTS, CHOPPED
- 1½ POUNDS ONIONS, CHOPPED
- 3 POUNDS CRACKED VEAL BONES, INCLUDING KNUCKLES
- 3 GARLIC CLOVES, PEELED
- 1 BOUQUET GARNI (2 SPRIGS PARSLEY, 1 BAY LEAF, 1 SPRIG FRESH THYME, AND 1 STALK CELERY, TIED IN A SQUARE OF CHEESECLOTH)
- SALT AND FRESHLY GROUND PEPPER

. . . .

GARNISH

- 1¾ POUNDS CARROTS, CUT IN 2-INCH LENGTHS
- 24 SMALL WHITE ONIONS, OR 1 POUND FROZEN, SMALL, WHITE ONIONS, THAWED
- 7 OUNCES GREEN BEANS
- 10½ OUNCES FROZEN PETITS POIS, THAWED
- 8 SMALL POTATOES, PEELED
- 2 TABLESPOONS FINELY CHOPPED FRESH PARSLEY OR FINES HERBES

TO PREPARE THE BEEF: In a large, heavy Dutch oven over medium-high heat, brown the meat in the oil on all sides. Set the meat aside, covered, add the carrots and onions to the pot, and sauté until lightly colored. Return the meat to the pot and add the bones, garlic, bouquet garni, and salt and pepper. Add enough water to cover the meat, bring to a boil, lower the heat, and simmer gently for 2½ hours, until the meat is very tender.

TO MAKE THE GARNISH: While the meat is cooking, prepare the vege-tables for garnish by steaming or blanching each vegetable separately until just tender. Refresh in cold water to stop cooking and to set the color. For the frozen peas, thaw but do not cook, since they have been blanched before freezing. Set aside the vegetables.

When the meat is tender, remove it from the pot and set aside, covered to keep warm. Strain the cooking liquid through a fine sieve into a saucepan. Discard the bones and vegetables. Return the liquid to heat and reduce the sauce to 4 cups. Adjust the seasonings.

Place the reserved garnish vegetables in the sauce and warm through over low heat. Carve meat into thick slices, place on a serving platter, and spoon the vegetables and sauce over the meat. Sprinkle with parsley or fines herbes.

SERVES 8 TO 10

Crème Caramel

[CARAMEL CUSTARD]

The long, slow cooking of this classic dessert produces a perfectly smooth and silky custard.

- 1 QUART MILK
- 2 VANILLA BEANS, SPLIT LENGTHWISE, OR 3 TEASPOONS VANILLA EXTRACT
- 2 CUPS SUGAR
- 3 TABLESPOONS WATER
- 1 DROP VINEGAR OR LEMON JUICE
- 8 LARGE EGGS
- YOLKS OF 4 LARGE EGGS
- SMALL PINCH SALT

In a large saucepan over low heat, scald the milk with the vanilla beans. Remove from the heat, cover, and steep for 30 minutes. Then remove the vanilla beans and discard.

Caramelize an 8-cup mold: Place ½ cup of the sugar, the water, and vinegar or lemon juice

CHEF PETIT'S CUSTARDY CRÈME CARAMEL IS LARGE ENOUGH TO SERVE EIGHT.

in a small saucepan and cook over high heat until golden. Carefully pour into the mold and tilt the mold to coat the bottom with caramel. Let the caramel harden.

Preheat the oven to 300°F.

Place the eggs, yolks, the 1½ cups remaining sugar, and salt in a bowl; whisk together until the mixture thickens and is pale yellow. Strain the milk into the egg mixture and stir it to blend. Pour the custard mixture very carefully into the previously caramelized mold.

Place the mold in a larger pan, place the pan on the oven rack, and fill the pan with hot water to come halfway up the mold. Bake 1½ to 2 hours, until the custard is set when a knife inserted in the center comes out clean.

Cool, then refrigerate. To serve, run a knife around the edge of the pan. Invert the mold onto a deep serving dish. The caramel will run out and fill the dish.

SERVES 6 TO 8

Compotiers de Boeuf à la Parisienne

[PARISIAN-STYLE COLD-BEEF SALAD]

2 POUNDS BONELESS CHUCK ROAST

1 BOUQUET GARNI (2 SPRIGS FRESH PARSLEY, 1 BAY LEAF, 1 SPRIG FRESH THYME, AND 1 STALK CELERY, TIED IN A SQUARE OF CHEESECLOTH)

SALT AND FRESHLY GROUND PEPPER

3 MEDIUM CARROTS, QUARTERED

3 LEEKS, WHITE PART ONLY, HALVED AND WASHED WELL

1 LARGE ONION, QUARTERED

½ CELERY ROOT, PEELED

3 ENVELOPES UNFLAVORED GELATIN

TOMATO, HARD-COOKED EGG, AND FINES HERBES, TO GARNISH

Place the meat, bouquet garni, and the salt and pepper in a large pot and cover with cold water. Bring to a boil and carefully skim the foam from the surface. Simmer the meat over low heat for 3 hours. Then add the vegetables and cook 2 hours longer.

Strain the broth through a cheesecloth, remove any fat, and return 5 cups of the broth to the pot. Dice the meat and vegetables. (There should be about 8 cups.) In a small saucepan bring 1 cup of the broth to boil and sprinkle in the gelatin, stirring until completely dissolved. Add this broth mixture to the 5 cups of broth. Stir in the meat and vegetables and place the pot over ice, stirring the mixture occasionally until liquid becomes syrupy.

Pour into a 12-cup ring mold and chill overnight. To serve, plunge the mold into hot water for several seconds and invert onto a round plate. Decorate with quarters of tomato and hard-cooked egg; sprinkle with fines herbes, and serve with Sauce Rémoulade (recipe follows).

SERVES 8 TO 10

. . . .

STEAMED VEGETABLES BRIGHTEN THE BOEUF À LA MODE (PAGE 70).

Sauce Rémoulade

[MUSTARD-MAYONNAISE SAUCE WITH CAPERS AND HERBS]

YOLK OF 1 LARGE EGG (SEE NOTE)

1 TABLESPOON DIJON-STYLE MUSTARD

1 CUP PEANUT OIL

SALT AND FRESHLY GROUND PEPPER

1 HARD-COOKED EGG, CHOPPED

4 CORNICHONS, CHOPPED

1 TABLESPOON SMALL CAPERS, DRAINED

2 TABLESPOONS FINELY CHOPPED FRESH PARSLEY, TARRAGON, AND CHIVES

Using a whisk, beat together the egg yolk and mustard. Add the oil drop by drop until the mixture thickens. Then add the remaining oil in a steady stream. Stir in the remaining ingredients.

MAKES ABOUT 1½ CUPS

NOTE: If you are concerned about health hazards from raw eggs, substitute 1 cup commercial mayonnaise for the yolk and the oil, whisk in the mustard, and then stir in the remaining ingredients.

Blanquette de Jarret de Veau

[BRAISED VEAL SHANK BLANQUETTE]

3- TO 4-POUND VEAL SHANK, IN ONE PIECE

½ LEMON

1 LARGE ONION, QUARTERED

2 MEDIUM CARROTS, QUARTERED

1 BOUQUET GARNI (2 SPRIGS FRESH PARSLEY, 1 BAY LEAF, 1 SPRIG FRESH THYME, AND ½ STALK CELERY, TIED IN A SQUARE OF CHEESECLOTH)

SALT AND FRESHLY GROUND PEPPER

12 SMALL MUSHROOMS, CLEANED AND TOSSED WITH 1 TABLESPOON LEMON JUICE

BENOÎT'S *BLANQUETTE* IS A PERENNIAL FAVORITE AMONG HABITUÉS.

. . . .

12 SMALL WHITE ONIONS

2 TABLESPOONS UNSALTED
BUTTER

¼ CUP ALL-PURPOSE FLOUR

¾ CUP CRÈME FRAÎCHE

Peel the thin silver skin from the veal shank and trim off any fat. Soak the veal overnight in cold water in the refrigerator. Pour off the water and rub the veal all over with the lemon. Place the veal in a large pot, cover with cold water, and bring to a boil. Meanwhile, bring about 1 quart of fresh water to a boil in a large pot and add the quartered onion, carrots, and bouquet garni. Drain the water from the veal and add it to the pot with the onion and carrots. Season with salt and pepper, lower heat, and simmer gently for about 2½ to 3 hours, until the veal is tender when pierced with a fork.

Remove the meat from the bone and cover to keep warm. Strain the liquid through a sieve and measure 2 cups of liquid to make the sauce. Add the mushrooms and onions and simmer for about 15 minutes, until the vegetables are tender. Remove with a slotted spoon and keep warm with the veal.

Melt the butter in a medium saucepan and whisk in the flour. Stirring constantly, cook the mixture 3 to 4 minutes, until it begins to color. Gradually whisk in the 2 cups of liquid and bring to a boil, stirring often. Lower the heat and simmer for 15 minutes, stirring occasionally.

Heat the crème fraîche in another medium saucepan and reduce it by half until very thick. Whisk the sauce mixture into the crème fraîche and adjust the seasoning. Slice the veal. Pour the sauce over the veal, mushrooms, and onions and serve with noodles or rice.

SERVES 3 TO 4

Marquise au Chocolat

[CHOCOLATE ALMOND
MOUSSE CAKE]

6 TABLESPOONS (¾ STICK)
UNSALTED BUTTER

4 TABLESPOONS WATER

3 TABLESPOONS KIRSCH

11 OUNCES SEMISWEET
CHOCOLATE, CHOPPED

YOLKS OF 3 LARGE EGGS

⅓ CUP SUGAR

1 ENVELOPE
UNFLAVORED GELATIN,
SOFTENED IN
2 TABLESPOONS WATER

WHITES OF 4 LARGE EGGS

5 TABLESPOONS SLIVERED
ALMONDS, TOASTED

3 DOZEN LADYFINGERS

2 CUPS CRÈME ANGLAISE
(PAGE 63)

Bring the butter, water, and kirsch to a boil in a medium heavy-bottomed saucepan. Remove from heat and stir in the chocolate until smooth. Place the egg yolks and 3 tablespoons of the sugar in the bowl of an electric mixer and beat 5 minutes on high speed, until very pale and thick. Stir in the chocolate mixture and the softened gelatin and return to the saucepan.

Cook over medium heat, stirring constantly, for about 10 minutes, until mixture is very hot. (Do not let boil or the yolks will curdle.) Set aside. Beat the egg whites with the remaining sugar until soft peaks form. Fold into the hot chocolate mixture. Place the bowl over ice and stir occasionally until the mixture thickens and chills. Fold in the almonds.

Line a 9 × 5-inch loaf pan with wax paper. Place a row of ladyfingers on the bottom of the pan, curved side down, and line the sides of the pan with ladyfingers. Spoon in half of the chocolate mixture and add a layer of ladyfingers. Spoon in the remaining chocolate and top with the remaining ladyfingers. Trim off the tops of the ladyfingers that protrude over the edge of the pan. Cover with wax paper and chill 4 hours or overnight before unmolding.

To serve, remove wax paper and invert onto a serving platter. Slice with a sharp thin-bladed knife. Serve covered with Crème Anglaise.

SERVES 8 TO 10

THE ELEGANT AMBIANCE OF BENOÎT FEATURES MARBLE COLUMNS, PALMS, AND AN ARRAY OF DESSERTS AND SALADS.

CHECKED TABLECLOTHS AND OLD-FASHIONED SENTIMENTS ON THE WALL AND MIRRORS SET THE MOOD AT D'CHEZ EUX.

Trois Salades du Chariot

Bisque de Homard

Pruneaux à l'Armagnac

·············

Moules Farcies Gratinées du Chef

Filet de Boeuf Poché à la Ficelle

Pamplemousse à la Menthe

D'CHEZ EUX

ining at D'Chez Eux (At Their Place) is an experience of plenty that begins as soon as you are seated on one of the wine-colored velour banquettes. A waiter, garbed in a distinctive blue-striped overblouse originally designed for professional horse dealers, arrives with stemmed glasses of a *kir au fraise* (white wine laced with strawberry liqueur). Accompanying the house apéritif are small servings of charcuterie, an oval tub of sweet butter, and a plateful of crusty whole wheat bread. Symbols of abundance are everywhere in this cheerful corner restaurant with its bright red awning and cherry-pink checked table-cloths. Chains of garlic, aged Bayonne hams, Auvergnat sausages, and a winsome carved pig hang from the beams; a jeroboam of armagnac graces the worn wood bar; large wicker baskets bristling with assorted charcuterie dominate a small serving table; and two rolling *chariots* (carts), each crowded with fifteen to twenty heavy orange casserole dishes, offer a dizzying choice of appetizers and desserts, perfect for the epicurean diner who may want to sample a little bit of everything.

D'Chez Eux is a sentimental favorite of mine. It was my first ex-perience of a "nice" Pari-sian restaurant after I ar-rived in France on a stu-dent exchange program in spring 1968. George

HEAPED WITH A VARIETY OF TOP-QUALITY DRY SAUSAGES, THE CHARCUTERIES
BASKETS AT D'CHEZ EUX CAN BE ORDERED AS A FIRST COURSE.

. . . .

Raymond, an expatriate colleague of my father's, invited me to lunch on a balmy early September day, and for me the meal was like a dream of Paris come true. The pretty tablecloths, the plush banquettes, the bustling, convivial atmosphere, the very sophisticated clientele, a distinguished escort . . . and the *chariots!* The waiter, amused to have a wide-eyed customer instead of one of his worldly habitués, heaped my plate with a selection of hors d'oeuvres: *salade de boeuf; céleri rémoulade*; ratatouille; calamari mayonnaise; a corn, artichoke, and pimiento salad; and tiny white mushrooms in a mustard cream sauce. For my main course I had the *poêlée de Saint-Jacques à l'échalote* (succulent sea scallops with their orange coral still attached, sautéed in butter and shallots and served still sizzling in an oval copper pan). The wine we drank was a fruity chilled Chiroubles, a delicious Beaujolais that is still the house wine. Dessert verged on gluttony as I requested a *dégustation* from the dessert *chariot* that required no less than two plates, and was accompanied, at the request of my host, by "*une*

belle montagne de crème fraîche."

On my first visit to D'Chez Eux, and for many visits thereafter, we were always greeted by Albert Court, smiling, pink-faced, and white-haired, who acquired the restaurant in 1963 after he had spent many years as director of Charlot 1er: Merveille de Mers, a seafood restaurant that used to close annually for the three months of the year without an *r*. What had once been a chauffeurs' and taxi drivers' café in the years after World War I, and then the dining room of a residential hotel after World War II, became, under Monsieur Court, a fashionable neighborhood bistro catering to diplomats from UNESCO, headquartered down the street; delegations from surrounding embassies; high-level staff from the nearby ministries of Health, the Navy, and the Post Office; and residents who lived in the graceful buildings of the elegant 7th *arrondissement.*

In the late 1960s and through the 1970s the tables were always full and reservations were at a premium. Business slowed somewhat in the 1980s, as it did for many traditional restaurants, when nouvelle

cuisine came into vogue. Today, with the renewed passion in Paris and elsewhere for classic *cuisine bourgeoise* that has gourmands disputing where one can find the best pot-au-feu or roast leg of spring lamb, the fortunes of D'Chez Eux are once again on the upswing.

Albert Court is retired now, spending much of his time at his house in Normandy, and the restaurant is under the guidance of his son, Jean-Pierre, a graduate of the elite Ecole Hôtelier de Lausanne. "Very little has changed in the almost three decades we've had the restaurant," notes Jean-Pierre. "We've kept our *chariots*, our baskets of charcuterie, and have maintained the *esprit de tradition* of our menu, with dishes like the cassoulet, the *fricassée de poulet fermier aux morilles* [sautéed farm chicken in a morel cream sauce], the *poule au pot*, and daily specials like our Filet de Boeuf Poché à la Ficelle [poached beef on a string], and our *filet mignon de veau Vieille France* [tender medallion of veal in a Calvados, cream, and mushroom sauce]. Our chef, François Casteleyn, has been with us since 1973. Just about the only thing that *has* changed are the shades on the little wall lamps. We removed the ones made out of sausage-casing and replaced them with fluted glass."

D'Chez Eux is a Paris classic—not *branché*, or "in," not world renowned, just a solidly established, family-run restaurant serving excellent, old-fashioned, well-loved

. . . .

OWNER JEAN-PIERRE COURT, FAR LEFT,
POSES WITH HIS STAFF.

fare to its well-heeled neighbors from the Avenue de Suffren, the Avenue de la Bourdonnais, the Avenue de Saxe, and the Boulevard de la Tour-Maubourg. The menus, designed and printed years before Paris telephone numbers went to eight digits in the mid-1980s, still bear the telephone number as it was when I first came to Paris, when the exchanges reflected the subscriber's neighborhood: Solférino 52-55. I have dined in many fine restaurants in France since my first experience at D'Chez Eux and enjoyed a number of memorable meals in Paris and the provinces. But few places warm my heart the way this familiar, unchanged old place does. Choosing my desserts from the *chariot*, with the tall crock of crème fraîche before me, I always hear the echo of George Raymond's voice, in his flawless French, directing the waiter to serve me *"une belle montagne."* This is my "petit madeleine."

Trois Salades du Chariot

[THREE SALADS FROM THE CHARIOT]

....

RATATOUILLE

½ CUP OLIVE OIL

1 POUND EGGPLANT, CUBED (ABOUT 6 CUPS)

¾ POUND GREEN BELL PEPPER, CUBED (ABOUT 2½ CUPS)

1 POUND ONIONS, CUBED (ABOUT 3 CUPS)

1 POUND ZUCCHINI, CUBED (ABOUT 3⅓ CUPS)

1½ POUNDS TOMATOES, CUBED (ABOUT 4 CUPS)

3 HEADS GARLIC, FINELY CHOPPED

2 TABLESPOONS FRESH CHERVIL

2 TABLESPOONS FRESH CHIVES

SALT AND FRESHLY GROUND PEPPER

Heat 2 tablespoons of the oil in a large skillet. In 4 batches, brown the eggplant, pepper, and onions, adding 2 tablespoons of the oil to the pan for each batch. Return the browned vegetables to the skillet. Add the zucchini, tomatoes, and garlic, and cook just until vegetables are tender. Let cool. Add the fresh herbs and season to taste.

SERVES 8 TO 10

....

SALADE DE CHAMPIGNONS

[MUSHROOM SALAD IN CREAM SAUCE]

1 POUND SMALL WHITE MUSHROOMS, STEMS REMOVED, SLICED THIN

JUICE OF ½ LEMON

½ CUP CRÈME FRAÎCHE

1 TABLESPOON PLUS 2 TEASPOONS DIJON-STYLE MUSTARD

¼ TEASPOON SALT

CHOPPED FRESH PARSLEY, FOR GARNISH (OPTIONAL)

Place the mushroom slices in a medium-size bowl. Sprinkle lemon juice over the slices and toss gently but well. In a separate small bowl, whisk together the crème fraîche, mustard, and salt.

Pour the crème fraîche sauce over the mushrooms and toss gently to coat completely. Chill for at least 1 hour. Garnish with chopped parsley, if desired.

SERVES 4

....

CÉLERI RÉMOULADE

[CELERY ROOT SALAD IN MUSTARD MAYONNAISE]

1 POUND CELERY ROOT (SEE NOTE), PEELED AND GRATED (ABOUT 3½ CUPS)

JUICE OF 1 LEMON

¼ CUP MAYONNAISE (PAGE 62, OR USE COMMERCIAL MAYONNAISE)

2 TABLESPOONS DIJON-STYLE MUSTARD

2 TABLESPOONS WATER

SALT AND FRESHLY GROUND PEPPER

Toss the celery root with the lemon juice to preserve the color. Combine the other ingredients and toss with the celery root. Chill in the refrigerator for an hour or two before serving.

SERVES 6

NOTE: Celery root, often called celeriac, is available primarily during winter.

....

FOR A SMALL SUPPLEMENT, A CUSTOMER MAY MAKE AN ENTIRE MEAL OUT OF A SELECTION OF APPETIZERS FROM THE ROLLING *CHARIOT*.

Bisque de Homard

[LOBSTER BISQUE]

4 1-POUND LIVE LOBSTERS

¼ CUP OLIVE OIL

1 MEDIUM ONION, DICED

2 MEDIUM CARROTS, DICED

1 LEEK, WHITE PART ONLY, DICED

½ CUP COGNAC

2 CUPS DRY WHITE WINE

2 CUPS WATER

1 TABLESPOON BUTTER, SOFTENED AND MIXED WITH 2 TABLESPOONS FLOUR

½ CUP CRÈME FRAÎCHE

Prepare the lobsters by cutting between head and body with a sharp knife, killing them instantly. If desired, remove and reserve the tomalley (the soft liver of the lobster) and set aside. Cut the bodies, heads, and feelers into small pieces. Remove the meat from the tail and claws and set aside.

Heat 3 tablespoons of the oil, add the lobster and the vegetables, and sauté for 10 minutes. Pour in 6 tablespoons of the cognac. Heat for 1 minute, and then carefully light with a match. When the flames subside, add the wine and water. Bring to a boil, then lower the heat and simmer for 30 minutes. Strain through a food mill, extracting as much liquid from the mixture and shells as possible. Return the broth to the heat. Stir in the butter and flour mixture, called a *roux*. Let simmer 10 minutes longer to thicken slightly. Add the reserved tomalley, if desired, blending into the sauce.

Heat the remaining oil in a large saucepan. Cut the reserved lobster meat into ½-inch pieces, add to the saucepan, and stir to coat with oil. Add the remaining cognac, light again, let flames subside, then

cook 1 minute longer. Add the soup. Correct the seasonings. Ladle into large soup bowls, then add a heaping tablespoon of crème fraîche to each serving.

SERVES 4

Pruneaux à l'Armagnac

[BRANDIED PRUNES]

This intoxicating recipe works equally well with a pound of dried apricots, substituting white wine for red, and a vanilla bean for the cinnamon stick.

1 POUND PRUNES

1 CINNAMON STICK

ABOUT ½ BOTTLE (2 CUPS) FULL-BODIED RED WINE (CAHORS, MADIRAN, BORDEAUX)

½ CUP PRUNE EAU-DE-VIE OR OTHER FRUIT-FLAVORED CLEAR LIQUEUR

¼ CUP ARMAGNAC

VANILLA ICE CREAM

In a ceramic bowl, combine the prunes and cinnamon stick with enough red wine to cover completely. Cover with plastic wrap and refrigerate overnight.

The next day, transfer the prunes and their liquid to a medium saucepan and bring to a boil over medium-high heat. Remove from the heat and let cool completely. Stir in the eau-de-vie.

Just before serving, heat a snifter of armagnac above a candle flame. When hot, tip the glass slightly and ignite the contents using a match. Pour the still-flaming armagnac atop each serving of prunes. Serve with rich vanilla ice cream.

SERVES 4

NOTE: If you doubt your ability to control flaming brandy, simply drizzle a tablespoon or so of armagnac over each bowl of prunes and serve.

MOULES FARCIES COME STRAIGHT FROM THE OVEN IN ESCARGOT DISHES.
....

Moules Farcies Gratinées du Chef

[STUFFED MUSSELS WITH HERB BUTTER]

2 DOZEN MUSSELS

1 CUP DRY WHITE WINE

1 CUP WATER

½ CUP (1 STICK) UNSALTED BUTTER

2 LARGE SHALLOTS (ABOUT 3 OUNCES), CHOPPED

1 SMALL GARLIC CLOVE, FINELY CHOPPED

1 TABLESPOON CHOPPED FRESH PARSLEY

YOLKS OF 2 LARGE EGGS

¼ CUP RICARD LIQUEUR

Preheat the oven to 425°F.

Scrub and debeard the mussels. Poach the mussels in the wine and water just until the shells open. Pry open the shells and discard the top shells or remove the mussels from the shells and place in ceramic escargot dishes. Set aside.

In a small saucepan, melt 2 tablespoons of the butter. Add the shallots and cook slowly for 5 minutes over very low heat. Add the remaining butter and melt. Add the garlic and parsley. Stir in the egg yolks and the liqueur and beat lightly until creamy.

Spoon the mixture into each shell, covering the mussels. If using the escargot dishes, spoon the sauce over each mussel. Place the dish in the oven until the filling is golden. Serve hot.

SERVES 4

Filet de Boeuf Poché à la Ficelle

[POACHED FILET OF BEEF ON A STRING]

· · · · · · · · · ·

SAUCE MOUSSELINE

YOLKS OF 3 LARGE EGGS

1 TABLESPOON WATER

1 TABLESPOON LEMON JUICE (MORE IF NEEDED)

SALT

2 TABLESPOONS COLD UNSALTED BUTTER

½ CUP (1 STICK) UNSALTED BUTTER, MELTED

FRESHLY GROUND PEPPER

¼ CUP HEAVY CREAM, WHIPPED

2 TO 3 TABLESPOONS PREPARED HORSERADISH

· · · · · · · · · ·

FILET MIGNON

3 MEDIUM CARROTS, DICED

1 LARGE TURNIP, CUBED

3 LEEKS, WHITES ONLY, CHOPPED

4 CUPS BEEF STOCK

1 1¾-POUND FILET MIGNON (ABOUT 7 OUNCES PER PERSON)

SALT AND FRESHLY GROUND PEPPER

TO MAKE THE SAUCE: In a small saucepan, beat the egg yolks for about 1 minute, until thick and sticky. Add the water, lemon juice, and salt, and beat for 30 seconds

more. Drop in 1 tablespoon of the cold butter, but do not beat in. Place the saucepan over very low heat and whisk the mixture until it thickens into a smooth cream, 1 to 2 minutes.

Remove from the heat and beat in the remaining tablespoon of cold butter. While whisking, slowly drizzle in the melted butter until the mixture thickens to the consistency of heavy cream, then pour in the rest of the butter. Correct the seasonings with salt, pepper, and lemon juice. Fold the whipped cream and the horseradish into the sauce just before serving. Pour the sauce into a serving dish.

TO PREPARE THE FILET: In a large pot, poach the carrots, turnip, and leeks in the beef stock for 15 minutes. Add the meat and braise for 5 minutes per pound for rare meat. Remove the meat and keep warm. Correct the seasoning of the stock.

Traditionally, this is served in 2 courses. The vegetables in the soup are the first course, and the meat sliced with the Sauce Mousseline are the second.

SERVES 4

Pamplemousse à la Menthe

[GRAPEFRUIT WITH MINT AND WHITE WINE]

This lovely, refreshing dessert would be the perfect finish to a rich and copious meal, or a nice addition to a brunch buffet. The recipe also works well substituting 8 fresh peaches for the grapefruit. Before serving, remove the mint sprigs and discard. Serve each portion garnished with a fresh mint sprig and, as they do at D'Chez Eux, a big crock of vanilla ice cream on the side.

4 PINK GRAPEFRUIT, PEELED AND SECTIONED, ALL MEMBRANES AND SEEDS REMOVED

4 TABLESPOONS SUGAR

4 SPRIGS FRESH MINT

ABOUT ½ BOTTLE (2 CUPS) DRY WHITE WINE, SUCH AS CHARDONNAY

Arrange the grapefruit slices in a ceramic bowl. Sprinkle with the sugar, then top with the mint sprigs. Pour enough white wine over the grapefruit to cover. Cover the bowl with plastic wrap and refrigerate overnight.

SERVES 4

· · · · · · · · · · ·

CAKE OR CANDIED FRUITS COMPLEMENT D'CHEZ EUX'S LIGHT, ASTRINGENT PAMPLEMOUSSE A LA MENTHE, ALSO SERVED WITH A DOLLOP OF VANILLA ICE CREAM.

THE NEIGHBORHOOD HAS CHANGED, BUT CHEZ GEORGES REMAINS A HAVEN OF CLASSIC BISTRO DISHES AND REFINED SERVICE.

CHEZ GEORGES

High-rise hotels and the Palais de Congrès, a mammoth convention center, dominate today's Porte Maillot, a gateway into and out of Paris at the border between the 16th and 17th *arrondissements*. A blur of cars battling for the right of way at the intersection, where five roads converge onto the Avenue de la Grande-Armée makes crossing the street an exercise in stress management even for the most sanguine of pedestrians. But in 1926 a bucolic little park occupied the site where the superstructures now stand. Through the shaded grounds wound a labyrinth of wide paths for horse-drawn buggies and strollers out for an afternoon promenade. The only structures taller than the trees were a Ferris wheel and a soaring platform that served as a launching pad for daredevil divers who jackknifed into deep tubs of water far below. Across the way from this leafy haven was a refined bistro newly established by Georges Mazarguil. The guests at the popular restaurant included not only the *haute bourgeoisie* neighbors but the leading sportsmen of the decade. Among the earliest patrons of Chez Georges were the boxer Georges Charpentier, the tennis champions Réné Lacoste and Jean Borotra, and a clique of *automobilistes* (car enthusiasts) drawn to the neighborhood by

ETCHED-GLASS EVOKES A GENTLER TIME
IN CHEZ GEORGES'S HISTORY.

. . . .

the Bugatti and Mercedes show-room-garages.

While the surrounding neighborhood changed dramatically, trading tranquillity and a gentle pace for quickened commercial vitality, Chez Georges persevered through the years, firmly entrenched at 273 Boulevard Péreire. Its marigold-yellow awnings still glow like a beacon for hungry neighbors and passersby, and after more than six decades the bistro continues to be a Mazarguil family affair. At the helm today is founder Georges's son, Roger Mazarguil, a tall, distinguished, silver-haired man who looks more like a revered member of the Sénat than a bistro *propriétaire*. His able second is manager Dominique Cler. Monsieur Roger, as the staff calls him in the classic bistro tradition, treasures his recollections of growing up during the restaurant's—and also his—first decade. "The early years were exciting ones at Chez Georges," he says. "There was a boom economy; people loved going out. And everyone who was anyone seemed to end up Chez Georges. There were *cinéastes* like Abel

Gance, surrealists like Jacques Prévert, and of course there were the *automobilistes*, the *aviateurs*, and the athletes." Chez Georges, which quickly developed a reputation as a sports hangout, was even an unofficial part of one competition. "When I was little," recalls Monsieur Roger, "there used to be an annual bicycle race from Paris to Bordeaux, starting from the Porte Maillot. And every year the racers came here early in the morning for a big breakfast of eggs and baguettes to fortify themselves before the race. As they left the tables they all stuffed their pockets with sugar to give them energy on the road."

"Mr. Mazarguil and his *cordon bleu*, Madame Françoise, will astonish you for your 25 or 30 francs," reads a 1932 restaurant guide, *Les Auberges de France*, sponsored by Escoffier. "The main courses are sliced and served before your eyes, which will be dazzled by the sporting-world clientele. . . . Very pleasant setting." While athletes no longer prevail at the tables Chez Georges, the setting of paneled walls, banquette tables covered with embossed white linens, and period details such as the handsome carved oak bar, the tiled floors, and the bentwood coatracks, is still *très agréable,*" and the house specialty is still succulent roasts sliced before your eyes.

Chez Georges's handwritten menu, with its Art Deco logo of athletes in silhouette, features classic bistro dishes prepared by chefs Pierre Banchet and Stéphane Dudek. An unusually large selection of appetizers—twenty-five to thirty—is offered to start off the meal, including five or six salads, terrines of salmon, chicken livers or rabbit, herring marinated or *à la crème*, Parma ham, and during the winter months a soul-warming *soupe aux choux*, a cabbage soup

simmered with bits of pork. Among the nine or ten mostly traditional main courses are the Haricot de Mouton (braised lamb with white beans), the Hachis Parmentier (a French shepherd's pie), *blanquette de veau* (veal stew in a white sauce), *coq au vin*, and *saumon à l'oseille* (poached salmon in a sorrel sauce). But the perennial favorites among habitués at both lunch and dinner are the juicy roasts—the *gigot d'agneau* (leg of lamb), and the *train de côtes de boeuf* (tender roast beef)—set on rolltop carts of brass and mahogany and sliced to order at your table. Accompanying the lamb is a small casserole of *flageolets fins*, the small, delicately flavored pale green beans traditionally served with a *gigot;* served with the beef is a golden-crusted *gratin dauphinois*, sliced potatoes baked in milk and cheese. To complement this satisfying fare is a small, well-chosen wine list offering a diverse and reasonably priced selection of reds, whites, and rosés, including the unofficial house wines, the Côtes de Brouilly, a Beaujolais chosen on the property, and a Quincy (pronounced *Can-SEE*), a dry white wine from the upper Loire Valley.

Standouts on the small, separate dessert menu are the Crêpe Soufflé au Coulis d'Abricot (billowing crêpes with an apricot sauce), the Sorbet Pommes Vertes au Calvados (green apple sorbet splashed with Calvados), and the *éclair géant*, an eye-popping chocolate or coffee eclair the size of a small baguette.

Over the last half-century, neither the menu nor the interior design has changed significantly Chez Georges. A storage room that once sheltered Allied aviators and members of the Resistance during World War II ("They slept on sacks of potatoes," recalls Monsieur Roger) is now the rear dining room; the oak bar was relieved of its zinc top by the Germans in the early 1940s; and the decor was subtly freshened several years ago by Paris restaurant designer Slavik. But essentially Chez Georges remains what it has always been—for the neighbors, a decorous and reliable bistro with a great deal of class, and for Monsieur Roger, a font of memory.

Salade Verte aux Fines Herbes

[GREEN SALAD WITH FRESH HERBS]

With a hearty main course, it is pleasant to start with a very light appetizer, such as a crisp green salad lightly flavored with fresh garden herbs.

- 1 SMALL HEAD BOSTON LETTUCE, TORN INTO LARGE PIECES
- 1 SMALL HEAD CURLY ENDIVE OR CHICORY, OR ANY OTHER SEASONAL LETTUCE, SUCH AS MÂCHE, LAMB'S EARS, OR RED-LEAF, BROKEN INTO LARGE PIECES

....

A GREEN SALAD IS OFFERED AMONG THE APPETIZERS.

- 4 TABLESPOONS PEANUT OIL
- 1 TABLESPOON WINE VINEGAR
- SALT AND FRESHLY GROUND PEPPER
- 1 TABLESPOON FINELY CHOPPED FRESH TARRAGON
- 1 TABLESPOON FINELY CHOPPED FRESH CHERVIL
- 1 TABLESPOON FINELY CHOPPED FRESH PARSLEY
- 4 TO 6 SPRIGS FRESH CHERVIL, CUT IN LARGE PIECES
- 6 CELERY LEAVES

Combine the greens in a large salad bowl. Whisk together the oil, vinegar, and the salt and pepper to taste in a bowl to make a vinaigrette sauce. Just before serving, pour the vinaigrette over the greens and sprinkle on the fresh herbs and the celery leaves. Toss gently, then divide onto 4 salad plates and serve.

SERVES 4

Hachis Parmentier

[SHEPHERD'S PIE]

Antoine Augustin Parmentier was an eighteenth-century French agronomist who heavily promoted the potato as a nutritious addition to the French diet. (It had been dismissed by the French as animal food until Parmentier's changed its image.) Many dishes today containing potatoes, such as Hachis Parmentier, are named in his honor.

- 1 POUND GROUND ROUND STEAK
- ¼ POUND FATTY BACON, BLANCHED AND FINELY CHOPPED
- 1 TABLESPOON VEGETABLE OIL
- 1 GARLIC CLOVE, CHOPPED
- 2 SHALLOTS, CHOPPED
- 1 MEDIUM ONION, CHOPPED
- 1 TABLESPOON CHOPPED FRESH PARSLEY
- 2 TABLESPOONS TOMATO PASTE
- 2 TABLESPOONS DRY WHITE WINE
- SALT AND FRESHLY GROUND PEPPER
- 1¾ POUNDS POTATOES, PEELED AND CUBED

CÔTES DE BROUILLY MARRIES WELL WITH HACHIS PARMENTIER.

....

- 3 TABLESPOONS UNSALTED BUTTER
- FRESHLY GRATED NUTMEG
- ⅓ CUP GRATED GRUYÈRE CHEESE

Brown the steak and bacon in the oil over high heat. Add the garlic, shallots, onion, parsley, tomato paste, wine, and salt and pepper. Stir and simmer, partially covered, for 2 hours, stirring occasionally.

Boil the potatoes in salted water until tender, for about 5 minutes. Drain, mash, and mix with 2 tablespoons of the butter. Season with additional salt and pepper, and the nutmeg.

Preheat the oven to 450°F.

Butter a shallow ovenproof 9 × 13-inch casserole or ovenproof glass baking dish. Spread a layer of potato on the bottom of the casserole. Place all of the meat mixture on the potato layer and cover with the remaining potato. Sprinkle with the cheese and dot with the remaining tablespoon of butter. Bake 20 minutes, until the cheese is melted and lightly browned and the dish is hot throughout.

SERVES 4

Sorbet Pommes Vertes au Calvados

[GREEN APPLE SORBET
WITH CALVADOS]

1 CUP WATER
1 CUP SUGAR
2 POUNDS GRANNY SMITH
APPLES, PEELED AND DICED
4 TABLESPOONS LEMON JUICE
CALVADOS
MINT LEAVES, FOR GARNISH

Bring the water and sugar to a boil in a saucepan. Cool the syrup and refrigerate until very cold. Toss the apples with the lemon juice. Place the sugar syrup and apples in a food processor or blender and puree. Scrape the apple mixture into an ice cream machine and freeze according to the manufacturer's directions.

Soften in the refrigerator before serving. Splash with some Calvados and garnish with mint leaves. Serve with crisp *crêpes dentelles*.

SERVES 8

. . . .

A *CRÊPE DENTELLE* DRESSES UP A DISH
OF GREEN APPLE SORBET.

SMOKED HADDOCK SALAD, A FAVORITE APPETIZER AT CHEZ GEORGES, GETS A NOTE
OF COLOR FROM A TOMATO ROSE.

. . . .

Salade de Haddock

[SMOKED HADDOCK SALAD]

1 SMALL HEAD BOSTON OR RED-
LEAF LETTUCE, TORN INTO LARGE
PIECES
1 SMALL HEAD CURLY ENDIVE OR
CHICORY, TORN INTO LARGE
PIECES
4 TABLESPOONS PEANUT OIL
1 TABLESPOON WINE VINEGAR
2 TEASPOONS DIJON-STYLE
MUSTARD
SALT AND FRESHLY GROUND
PEPPER
1 POUND SMOKED HADDOCK,
SLICED VERY THIN
1 LEMON, SLICED IN THIN
ROUNDS, THEN HALVED
4 SMALL RED-RIPE TOMATOES,
PEELED AND WITH SOME
FLESH CUT INTO A
CONTINUOUS STRIP

Combine the lettuce and chicory in a large salad bowl. Whisk together the oil, vinegar, mustard, and salt and pepper in a medium bowl to make a vinaigrette. Pour the sauce over the greens and toss well.

Divide the greens onto 4 individual salad plates. Arrange 4 to 6 slices of the smoked haddock over the greens, then decorate the border of each plate with the lemon slices. Wind the tomato peels into 4 rosettes and arrange one atop the center of each salad. Serve immediately.

SERVES 4

Haricot de Mouton

[BRAISED LAMB
WITH WHITE BEANS]

This savory dish tastes even better on the second day.

11 OUNCES DRIED WHITE BEANS,
SOAKED IN COLD WATER
OVERNIGHT
1 BOUQUET GARNI (1 SPRIG
EACH THYME AND PARSLEY AND
1 BAY LEAF, TIED IN A SQUARE
OF CHEESECLOTH)
1 MEDIUM ONION, STUDDED WITH
A WHOLE CLOVE

1 MEDIUM CARROT, CHOPPED

2 POUNDS LAMB SHOULDER, CUT
INTO 1½-INCH PIECES

SALT AND FRESHLY GROUND
PEPPER

SUGAR

2 TABLESPOONS OIL

3 TABLESPOONS ALL-PURPOSE
FLOUR

2 CUPS DRY WHITE WINE

1 TABLESPOON TOMATO PASTE

2 RIPE TOMATOES,
QUARTERED

4 GARLIC CLOVES, CRUSHED

1 SPRIG PARSLEY

1 SPRIG THYME

½ BAY LEAF

Drain the water from the beans. Place the beans in a large heavy-bottomed saucepan with the bouquet garni, onion, and carrot. Cover with water, bring to a boil, cover, and simmer 1 hour.

Sprinkle the lamb pieces with the salt, pepper, and sugar. Heat the oil in a skillet and brown the lamb. Place the lamb in a casserole over medium heat and sprinkle with the flour, stirring for several minutes. Add the remaining ingredients and bring to a boil. Cover and simmer for 1 hour.

. . . .

THE ART DECO MENU SITS BESIDE A
SERVING OF HARICOT DE MOUTON.

Drain any liquid from the beans, discard the bouquet garni, and add the beans to the lamb. Simmer until the lamb is tender, about 45 minutes more. Correct the seasoning. Degrease the sauce and serve lamb and beans heaped together.

SERVES 8

Crêpe Soufflé au Coulis d'Abricot

[SOUFFLÉED CRÊPES
WITH APRICOT SAUCE]

. . . .

CRÊPES

½ CUP ALL-PURPOSE FLOUR

¼ CUP SUGAR

PINCH SALT

2 LARGE EGGS

⅔ CUP MILK

1 TABLESPOON BUTTER

. . . .

FILLING

⅔ CUP MILK

½ VANILLA BEAN

YOLKS OF 2 LARGE EGGS

¼ CUP SUGAR

1½ TABLESPOONS ALL-PURPOSE
FLOUR

WHITES OF 4 LARGE EGGS

. . . .

APRICOT SAUCE

15 OUNCES (1 CAN) APRICOT
HALVES IN HEAVY SYRUP

3 TABLESPOONS LEMON JUICE

TO MAKE THE CRÊPES: Mix the ingredients with a whisk until smooth. Let mixture sit 30 minutes before using. Oil a 7-inch nonstick skillet, warm over medium-high heat, and swirl about 3 tablespoons of batter over the bottom of the pan. Cook over medium-high heat until the crêpe is set and the edges are lightly browned. Loosen with a thin spatula and turn the crêpe to

EACH CRÊPE SOUFFLÉ AU COULIS
D'ABRICOT IS MADE TO ORDER.

. . . .

brown on the other side for about 30 seconds. Slide onto a plate and repeat the procedure, stacking the finished crêpes and setting aside.

TO MAKE THE FILLING: Scald the milk with the vanilla bean. In a small saucepan, beat the yolks with the sugar and flour and gradually beat in the hot milk. Return the mixture to heat and bring to a boil, stirring continuously. Remove the vanilla bean and let the mixture cool completely, placing a sheet of wax paper on the surface to prevent a skin from forming. Beat the egg whites until firm and fold them into the filling mixture.

TO MAKE THE SAUCE: Drain the apricots, reserving 3 tablespoons of the syrup. Puree the apricots, reserved syrup, and lemon juice in a food processor or blender. Chill.

Preheat the oven to 450°F.

Butter a cookie sheet. Place each crêpe on a cookie sheet and spoon some of the filling on each crêpe. Fold the crêpe over the filling as if for a turnover. Bake about 7 minutes, until the crêpes are puffed. Serve with the sauce.

SERVES 6 (12 CRÊPES)

EGIONALS

Le Restaurant Bleu

. . . .

Au Pont Marie

. . . .

L'Auberge Pyrénées-Cévennes (Chez Philippe)

THE BLUE COLOR SCHEME OF THE RESTAURANT BLEU BEGINS AT THE FRONT DOOR.

LE RESTAURANT BLEU

The diminutive Restaurant Bleu announces itself boldly from more than a block away: the cheerful azure-blue façade stands in striking contrast to its sober gray neighbors along the rue Didot in this quiet residential area near Montparnasse. In keeping with its name, the restaurant is a palette of blues, outside and in. Behind the crocheted curtains that soften the light from the street, pale blue walls form a serene backdrop for a decor and a cuisine that glorify the Aveyron, the sunny, rustic *département* bordering the Auvergne region in south central France.

A timeless quality that marks many Paris bistros distinguishes the Restaurant Bleu as well. Little has changed here since 1935 when the restaurant opened. The ambiance is one of provincial charm, with bistro tables from the turn of the century covered with soft blue table linen, then draped with crocheted lace. Decorating the walls are rural, handcrafted *objets*, farm implements, regional posters, and a col-lection of carved-horn—handled knives from the Aveyron. Tucked in a corner are a pair of quaint wooden *sabots* with pointed toes worn for years by the shepherd father of Elie Bousquet, the current chef-owner, who runs the Restaurant Bleu along with his wife,

OWNER ELIE BOUSQUET IS THE ONLY CHEF IN THE NARROW BUT WELL-ORGANIZED
KITCHEN, WHICH HAS CHANGED LITTLE SINCE THE 1930S.

. . . .

Hélène, and their son, Gérard.

The establishment was founded as the Restaurant Tanqueray by Victor Bousquet, Elie Bousquet's uncle, who orchestrated his nephew's arrival from the provinces after World War II. "We were a very large family," recounts Chef Bousquet, "and there were very few opportunities for making a living in the Aveyron. So when I was a teenager, my uncle sent for me to work in his restaurant. I started as a *plongeur* [dishwasher], then worked my way up to a waiter, then assistant chef, then chef. In 1964 I was able to buy the restaurant." Shortly after taking command, the Bousquets noted that their property was in dire need of a fresh coat of paint. "We painted the walls a very light blue," says Hélène, "and the fifty-year-old façade a brighter, more striking blue. Once we finished, it became very obvious that our *restaurant bleu* should become *the* Restaurant Bleu!"

Chef Bousquet, a reserved and gentle man, cooks alone over an antique coal stove in his narrow, immaculate, tiled kitchen. The recipes he favors, and which high-light his menu, are as much a nostalgic homage to his native region as is the decor. Among the dishes Chef Bousquet presents daily, or seasonally, are a Salade du Berger, (shepherd's salad), with melted cheese and Bayonne ham; Saucisse Sèche à l'Huile en Salade (green salad with dry sausage preserved in oil); Truffade des Burons (shepherd's potato and cheese puree), a hearty entree; Rouelle de Veau Braisée aux Cèpes (braised veal with cèpe mushrooms), only available in the fall; grilled Charolais beef; and a *confit d'oie* (preserved goose casserole). The Bousquets offer a selection of Cahors wines that make robust companions for these rustic specialties.

Not a well-known restaurant even among Paris gourmands, the Restaurant Bleu has nevertheless garnered a rather noteworthy roster of diners. Among those crossing the bright blue threshold have been Valérie Giscard d'Estaing, the former president of France; Jacques Chirac, the mayor of Paris; Jean-Claude Lattès, the editor-in-chief of Hachette Publishers; and a "Madame Rockefeller." The old-est and most faithful customer, a bachelor businessman who lives in the building, and now in his late eighties, dined *chez* Bousquet every night for fifty years. When he retired he came for both lunch *and* dinner. These days, if he's too tired to come down, dinner is sent up.

The Bousquet's establishment has long been a favorite as well of the artistic community that populates this Montparnasse backwater, historically a *quartier* for the creative avant-garde. In the 1950s, while Elie Bousquet was still a waiter, the Giacometti brothers, Alberto and Diego, were among the neighborhood artists who used to dine here frequently. Chef Bousquet recalls them well, but with a touch of chagrin. "It was an era when we were still using paper tablecloths," he says. "Diego and Alberto used to come every day, and while they were eating and talking, they would draw all over the paper, sketching ideas, doodles, explaining a work in progress. And as soon as they'd paid their bill and were out the door, I would go over to the table, gather up the paper, and throw it away."

. . . .

TWO COAL SCUTTLES STAND READY TO
FUEL THE OLD-FASHIONED STOVE.

Salade du Berger

[SHEPHERD'S SALAD]

4 SLICES CRUSTY ITALIAN BREAD
OR ROUND FRENCH PEASANT
BREAD

2 SMALL ROUND, FRESH SHEEP'S
CHEESES, ½ POUND EACH

1 HEAD BOSTON LETTUCE, TORN
IN LARGE PIECES

1 HEAD CURLY ENDIVE OR
CHICORY, TORN IN LARGE PIECES

3 TABLESPOONS OLIVE OIL

1 TABLESPOON RED WINE
VINEGAR

FRESHLY GROUND PEPPER

2 SLICES PARMA, BAYONNE, OR
PROSCIUTTO HAM, IN STRIPS

Preheat the oven to 325°F.

Toast the bread in the oven. Cut the cheese into 4 slices and place 1 slice on each toast. Bake for about 9 minutes, until the cheese melts.

Whisk the oil, vinegar, and pepper together and toss with the greens. Place the greens on 4 salad plates. Strew the ham over the greens. Place the cheese toasts on each salad and serve.

SERVES 4

∙∙∙∙∙∙∙∙∙∙∙∙∙

SHEEP'S CHEESE (FOR SALADE DU
BERGER) RESEMBLES CAMEMBERT.

CROCHETED LACE OVER BLUE LINEN SETS THE STAGE FOR THE ROUELLE DE VEAU
BRAISÉE AUX CÈPES.

∙∙∙∙∙∙∙∙∙∙∙∙∙

Rouelle de Veau Braisée aux Cèpes

[BRAISED VEAL SHANK WITH
CÈPE MUSHROOMS]

3 TABLESPOONS VEGETABLE OIL

1 VEAL SHANK (ABOUT
2 POUNDS) CUT INTO
4 HORIZONTAL 1½- TO 2-INCH-
THICK OSSOBUCO SLICES

2 CUPS BEEF STOCK,
PREFERABLY HOMEMADE

4 MEDIUM CARROTS, CUT IN
2 × ½-INCH STICKS

SALT AND FRESHLY GROUND
PEPPER

¼ POUND SALT PORK, SLICED
¼ INCH THICK AND CUT INTO
1 × ¼-INCH STRIPS

1 POUND CÈPE OR CULTIVATED
MUSHROOMS, CLEANED AND
SLICED

2 TABLESPOONS CHOPPED FRESH
PARSLEY

In a large, deep, covered skillet, heat 2 tablespoons of the oil and brown the veal on all sides, for 8 to 10 minutes, over high heat. Remove the veal to a plate. Pour off the fat from the skillet and discard.

Deglaze the skillet with the broth, scraping up any brown bits. Add the carrots and cook over medium heat, covered, for about 5 minutes. Return the veal to the skillet, spooning the carrots over it. Sprinkle with the salt and pepper. Cover and simmer 40 to 50 minutes, until tender when pierced with a fork, turning the veal once after 20 minutes.

About 15 minutes before serving the veal, in a medium-size skillet, heat the remaining 1 tablespoon oil until hot but not smoking. Add the salt pork, reduce the heat to low, and cook the salt pork for about 10 minutes, until golden. Add the mushrooms, raise the heat to medium, and cook about 3 minutes, until tender, adding a small amount of oil if the mushrooms and salt pork begin to stick to the skillet. Sprinkle with the parsley.

On each of 4 dinner plates place 1 slice of veal. Spoon the carrots and then some of the mushroom mixture around each slice, and then pour some of the veal cooking liquid over each. Serve immediately.

SERVES 4

THE TIMELESS AMBIANCE OF THE RESTAURANT BLEU CREATES AN OLD-FASHIONED BISTRO MOOD.

Gourmandise du Chef

[CHEF'S PEACHES-AND-BERRY ICE CREAM TREAT]

· · · · · · · · · ·

COOKIES

2 LARGE EGGS

1 CUP GRANULATED SUGAR

¼ TEASPOON SALT

2 CUPS ALL-PURPOSE FLOUR

½ CUP (1 STICK) LIGHTLY SALTED BUTTER, AT ROOM TEMPERATURE

½ TEASPOON LEMON ZEST

· · · · · · · · · ·

BLACKBERRY SAUCE

2 CUPS FRESH BLACKBERRIES (SEE NOTE)

1 CUP CONFECTIONERS' SUGAR

· · · · · · · · · ·

ASSEMBLY

3 RIPE PEACHES, PEELED, PITTED, AND SLICED THIN

1 QUART CASSIS OR BLACKBERRY ICE CREAM (SEE NOTE)

½ CUP CRÈME FRAÎCHE

TO MAKE THE COOKIES: Preheat the oven to 400°F.

In a mixing bowl, beat together the eggs, sugar, and salt until a frothy lemon yellow. With a large wooden spoon, mix in the flour, butter, and lemon zest. Stir until all the ingredients are well blended.

On a floured work surface, with a floured rolling pin, roll the dough out to ¼-inch thickness. With a round cookie cutter or a small juice glass about 2½ inches in diameter, cut out the cookies and place on a greased cookie sheet. Bake for about 20 minutes, until golden. Cool on a rack. Serve immediately or store in a tin cookie box for up to a week. Makes 12 to 16 cookies.

TO MAKE THE SAUCE: In a food processor, process the blackberries for 5 seconds, until the fruit is fragmented but not quite pureed. Put the fruit into a strainer set over a bowl and press out all of the juice. Add the sugar to the bowl and stir well until the sugar dissolves. Refrigerate until needed or use immediately.

TO ASSEMBLE THE GOURMANDISE: Arrange the peach slices in a circle around the periphery of each dish, overlapping them slightly. Place a generous scoop of ice cream in the center of the peaches. Spoon ½ cup of blackberry sauce over the peaches. Top each scoop of ice cream with a tablespoon of crème fraîche, then insert a cookie at an angle into the crème fraîche. Serve immediately.

SERVES 4

NOTE: If fresh blackberries are not available for the sauce, use ½ cup of blackberry fruit spread, such as Polaner's All-Fruit. In a small saucepan, combine the spread with 2 tablespoons of water. Over low heat, stirring frequently, melt the jelly into a smooth sauce. Remove from heat and serve at room temperature.

If neither cassis nor blackberry ice cream is available, substitute ½ cup black currant preserves mixed with 1 quart vanilla ice cream and refrozen.

Saucisse Sèche à l'Huile en Salade

[GREEN SALAD WITH DRY SAUSAGE PRESERVED IN OIL]

· · · · · · · · · ·

SAUSAGE

2 POUNDS MILD DRY SAUSAGE, SUCH AS ABRUZZI DRY ITALIAN SAUSAGE OR SMALL SOPPRESSATA, NO MORE THAN 2 INCHES IN DIAMETER, SLICED IN ¼-INCH ROUNDS

½ TEASPOON BLACK PEPPERCORNS

3 GARLIC CLOVES (OPTIONAL)

5 CUPS PEANUT OR OLIVE OIL

· · · · · · · · · ·

SALAD

3 TABLESPOONS OLIVE OIL

1 TABLESPOON RED WINE VINEGAR

SALT AND FRESHLY GROUND PEPPER

1 HEAD BOSTON LETTUCE, BROKEN INTO LARGE PIECES

TO PREPARE THE SAUSAGE: Layer the sausage, peppercorns, and garlic cloves, if used, in a tall, wide-

· · · · · · · · · · · ·

DRY SAUSAGES PRESERVED IN OIL CAN BE STOCKED IN THE PANTRY TO BE SERVED AT IMPROMPTU COCKTAIL GATHERINGS WITH TOASTED BAGUETTE ROUNDS.

mouth 2-quart jar. Pour in the oil to cover the sausages generously. Close the jar tightly and store on a shelf in a cool spot for at least 1 month. Serve as needed. As the sausage is used, the oil can be used in salad dressing or for cooking.

Remove 4 slices of sausage per person from the jar, then dab with a paper towel to remove excess oil. TO MAKE THE SALAD: In a salad bowl whisk together the oil, vinegar, and the salt and freshly ground pepper. Add the lettuce and toss.

Divide onto 4 salad plates. Arrange the sausage slices on top of the lettuce. Serve with fresh, crusty bread and unsalted butter.

SERVES 4

Truffade des Burons

[POTATOES AND CHEESE PUREE, SHEPHERD STYLE]

3 TABLESPOONS PEANUT OIL

2 POUNDS POTATOES, PEELED AND SLICED ¼ INCH THICK

. . . .

CHEF BOUSQUET PREPARES TRUFFADE DES BURONS IN A TEMPERED IRON POT.

14 OUNCES FRESH TOMME DE CANTAL, OR IF UNAVAILABLE, A FROMAGE DES PYRÉNÉES, CUT IN ½-INCH CUBES

½ CUP FINELY CHOPPED FRESH PARSLEY

3 GARLIC CLOVES, MINCED

SALT AND FRESHLY GROUND PEPPER

In a 12-inch skillet, heat the oil until hot. Spread the potatoes evenly in the pan. Sauté, uncovered, over medium heat, for about 25 minutes, until cooked through and light golden, stirring occasionally.

Meanwhile, in a small bowl, toss together the cheese, parsley, and garlic. Sprinkle with the salt and pepper. Reduce the heat under the skillet to low. Stir the cheese mixture into the potatoes in the skillet, stirring briskly and constantly until melted, about 10 minutes. (The mixture should have the consistency of mashed potatoes.) Spoon onto a warm plate and serve immediately.

SERVES 4

Flan aux Poires

[PEAR FLAN]

4 CUPS MILK

6 LARGE EGGS

1 CUP VANILLA SUGAR (SEE DIRECTORY), OR 1 CUP SUGAR AND ½ VANILLA BEAN OR 1 TEASPOON VANILLA EXTRACT

¾ CUP SUGAR

¼ CUP WATER

2 PEARS, ANJOU OR BARTLETT, PEELED, CORED, AND CUT IN ½-INCH DICE

Preheat the oven to 350°F.

In a heavy saucepan, scald the milk. (Add the vanilla bean to the milk if vanilla sugar is not avail-

PEAR FLAN TEMPTS DINERS FROM A LONG SIDEBOARD.

. . . .

able.) Remove from heat. (Discard the vanilla bean if used.)

In a medium bowl, whisk the eggs with the vanilla sugar until pale; then pour into the milk, stirring constantly. Cover the custard and set aside.

Sprinkle the sugar evenly over the bottom of a heavy saucepan. Sprinkle on the water. Melt over medium heat, then continue to heat until caramelized. Do not stir. When the caramel is a medium amber color, remove from heat and pour over the bottoms and up the sides of eight 10-ounce custard cups, swirling the cups to cover.

Arrange the diced pears on the bottom of each custard cup. Pour the custard mixture over the pears. Arrange the cups in a bain-marie or in a large pan with hot water halfway up the outsides of the custard cups. Bake in the center of the oven for 40 to 45 minutes, until golden brown. Let cool on a rack in the bain-marie or pan for 30 minutes. Serve at room temperature. Extra servings can be refrigerated and served the next day.

SERVES 8

THE CURVING BAR AT AU PONT MARIE ONCE SERVED SAILORS AND FISHERMEN FROM THE BOATS THAT PLIED THE SEINE.

AU PONT MARIE

The two arms of the Seine clasp the Ile-Saint-Louis in a shimmering embrace that holds it apart from both the Right and Left banks. Barely 800 yards long, the Ile-Saint-Louis is lodged in the geographic heart of Paris, yet the residents of the island have long fancied themselves as separate. As little as twenty-five years ago, there were old *insulaires* (islanders), as they referred to themselves, who talked about "going to Paris" when they left the Ile by one of its six bridges to visit "the continent."

Along the four quais that encircle this village—the somber, shaded quai de Bourbon and the quai d'Anjou, facing the Right Bank, and the sun-washed quai de Bethune and the quai d'Orléans, facing the Left Bank—classic postcard images of Paris spring to life. Lovers embrace under an arch of the Pont Marie as a *bateau-mouche* glides by; painters and fishermen, so still they appear to be frozen in time, dot the riverbanks; towering poplars partially shade the façades of seventeenth-century buildings rendered luminous by the soft white light reflected off the water. Integral to this enchanting scene is a small and homey bistro, Au Pont Marie, beloved by *insulaires* and rediscovered daily by strollers on the quai de Bourbon, intrigued by its wine-red,

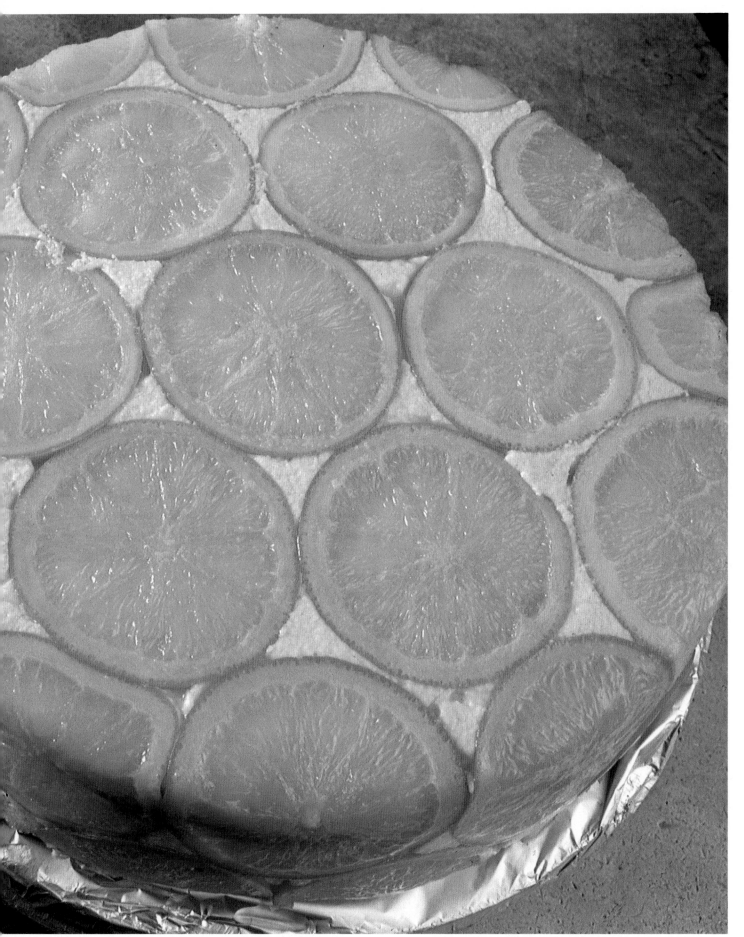

BOTH SPECTACULAR AND DELICIOUS, THE GÂTEAU À L'ORANGE IS A SPECIAL-OCCASION DESSERT.

AU PONT MARIE WAS ONCE LE BAR DES PÊCHEURS.

. . . .

turn-of-the-century façade.

The classified building that Au Pont Marie calls home was built, as were most structures on the Ile, in the mid-seventeenth century as part of an early urban development project headed by architect Christophe Marie and sanctioned by Louis XIII. The restaurant occupies what were once the stables of a grand mansion. By the late nineteenth century, the horse stalls had become the site of Le Bar des Pêcheurs, serving sailors and fishermen from the boats that used to dock along the Seine. After the turn of the century, the bar evolved into a simple *café-charbon* where many *insulaires* came to purchase their coal along with a simple meal. After almost seven decades as a *bougnat* for the island's working class and artistic community, the café was purchased in 1975 by Magali and Jean Griffoul, the current owners, who renovated the ancient interior.

Neighbors on the eight little streets of the Ile-Saint-Louis and office workers and merchants from the Marais district on the Right Bank crowd the restaurant at lunchtime, often waiting patiently at the bar until one of the little tables with red cloths and paper covers is vacated. In a setting as rustic and provincial as the food, with burlap-covered walls, hand-hewn beams, and wrought-iron wall sconces, diners enjoy a repertoire of dishes that might well be prepared by a Rouergate *grand-mère* on a Sunday afternoon. The menu offers choices among several savory salads, such as the Salade Landaise (foie gras and confit of chicken salad), the *salade aux lentilles et gésiers* (warm lentil salad topped with crisp duck giblets), or the *salade périgourdine* (salad with foie gras and strips of smoked duck filet); and sumptuous main-course Chou Farci à l'Auvergnat (stuffed cabbage Auvergnat style).

Au Pont Marie is an exclusive Griffoul family affair. While Magali and Jean are out front—she as hostess, he tending bar and dealing with volatile delivery men—and their daughter Laurence helps out as waitress, son Jean-Charles—moody and reserved but highly talented—presides in the minuscule kitchen. A born chef, as his mother describes him, to whom cooking came early and naturally, Jean-Charles trained in the kitchen of the highly respected Dodin-Bouffant before taking over as chef of the family enterprise at the age of eighteen, in the early 1980s. "He should be in a *grand restaurant* where he could express himself," says Magali, "but for the time being we're very lucky to have him with us." While everything at Au Pont Marie is as good and as copious as it should be, the big, round, exquisite tarts, displayed on the zinc counter to tantalize every arriving client, are in a realm by themselves. Every morning Jean-Charles creates succulent, seasonal tarts of apple-and-raisin, pear, *reine-claude* (greengage plum), blueberry, or cherry—some crumble-crusted, some glazed. And then, of course, there's his signature Gâteau à l'Orange, its vivid circlets of juicy orange brightening the somber bar like a cluster of little suns. Lavished with patience and love, these desserts testify to a talent that perhaps should be given freer rein.

Soupe de Nadaillac

[FRESH VEGETABLE SOUP]

1 CUP DRIED WHITE BEANS

10 CUPS WATER

3 MEDIUM TURNIPS, CUBED

3 MEDIUM CARROTS, SLICED

1 GREEN CABBAGE HEART, CUBED

1 TABLESPOON RENDERED GOOSE FAT (SEE NOTE)

SALT AND FRESHLY GROUND PEPPER

Simmer the beans in the water for about 1 hour, until they are just tender. Add the remaining vegeta-

GOOSE FAT ENRICHES A SIMPLE SOUP.

. . . .

bles and cook about 30 minutes longer. Stir in the goose fat and season to taste. Ladle and serve.

SERVES 8

NOTE: This simple soup from southwest France depends entirely on the goose fat for its fine flavor. If you cannot find rendered goose fat, use rendered chicken fat. See Directory for mail-order sources.

Magret de Canard au Poivre Vert

[DUCK BREAST WITH GREEN PEPPERCORNS]

4 LARGE DUCK BREASTS, ABOUT 7 TO 8 OUNCES EACH

½ CUP VEAL STOCK

½ CUP CRÈME FRAÎCHE

2 TABLESPOONS MASHED GREEN PEPPERCORNS

SALT

Preheat the oven to 475°F.

Place the duck breasts on a baking sheet, prick the skin with a fork, and roast for 20 minutes. Remove the breasts and keep them

warm. Skim off the fat and deglaze the roasting pan with the veal stock.

Pour stock into a saucepan and add the crème fraîche and green peppercorns. Cook about 10 minutes over medium heat, until the sauce has thickened slightly. Adjust the seasonings. Strain the sauce.

To serve, cut the duck breasts into thin slices against the grain and cover with the sauce. Serve with sliced potatoes sautéed until brown in goose fat (see Directory for sources).

SERVES 4

Gâteau à l'Orange

[GLAZED ORANGE BAVARIAN CAKE]

. . . .

GLAZED ORANGE SLICES

2¾ CUPS SUGAR

3 CUPS WATER

4 SEEDLESS ORANGES, SLICED THIN CROSSWISE

. . . .

CAKE

6 LARGE EGGS

⅔ CUP SUGAR

1 CUP ALL-PURPOSE FLOUR

2 TABLESPOONS UNSALTED BUTTER, MELTED

. . . .

ORANGE BAVARIAN CREAM

2 CUPS MILK

YOLKS OF 5 LARGE EGGS

10 TABLESPOONS SUGAR

1½ ENVELOPES UNFLAVORED GELATIN, SOFTENED IN 2 TABLESPOONS WATER

½ TEASPOON VANILLA EXTRACT

2 TABLESPOONS COINTREAU OR OTHER ORANGE-FLAVORED LIQUEUR

1 CUP HEAVY CREAM

TO GLAZE THE ORANGE SLICES: Bring the sugar and water to a boil in a large pot. Add the oranges, lower the heat, and simmer for 2½ hours. Remove from the heat. Let the oranges cool in the syrup overnight.

TO MAKE THE CAKE: Preheat oven to 350°F. Butter and flour a 10-inch springform pan.

Beat the eggs and sugar with an electric mixer for 10 minutes, until very thick and pale. Gradually fold

. . . .

ROAST DUCK BREASTS ARE SERVED RARE WITH SLICED POTATOES SAUTÉED IN DUCK FAT.

in the flour. Fold one-fourth of the batter into the melted butter, then fold the butter mixture into the remaining batter. Spoon the batter evenly into the prepared cake pan. Bake in the center of the oven for about 35 minutes, until a cake tester or toothpick inserted in the center of the cake comes out clean. Cool on a wire rack.

Run a knife around the edge of the pan to release the cake. Remove the sides and the bottom of the pan. Trim any crisp edges and slice the cake horizontally into 3 thin layers (see Note).

TO MAKE THE ORANGE BAVARIAN CREAM: In a medium saucepan, heat the milk to simmering. In a bowl, beat the yolks with 9 tablespoons of the sugar until well combined. Gradually beat in the hot milk. Stir in the softened gelatin. Return the mixture to the saucepan and cook over low heat, stirring constantly with a wooden spoon for about 10 minutes, until the mixture thickens enough to coat the back of a spoon. Do not let boil or the eggs will curdle. Stir in the vanilla and Cointreau. Place the saucepan over a bowl of ice and stir until the mixture mounds. In a bowl, softly whip the cream with the remaining tablespoon of sugar, then carefully fold it into the chilled Bavarian mixture.

To assemble, line a 10-inch springform pan with plastic wrap, leaving a 5-inch overhang all around. Drain the orange slices and reserve the syrup. Choose the largest slices and place them in a decorative pattern on the bottom and sides of the pan. Finely chop the remaining oranges and fold into the Bavarian cream.

Spoon one-third of the Bavarian cream over the oranges. Place 1 layer of the cake over the Bavarian cream and brush with some of the reserved syrup. Repeat twice with layers of the cream, cake, and syrup. Cover with plastic wrap.

BISTRO FARE FREQUENTLY INCLUDES *SALADES TIÈDES* (WARM SALADS).

. . . .

Place a 9-inch cake pan on top of the cake and put a 2-pound weight in the center of the pan. Refrigerate for at least 4 hours.

Remove the weighted pan and plastic wrap. Invert the cake onto a serving platter. Remove the sides and bottom of the pan and peel off the plastic wrap. Slice with a very sharp knife.

SERVES 12 TO 16

NOTE: The cake may be prepared several days in advance, wrapped well in plastic wrap or kept frozen. If frozen, unwrap before thawing.

Salade Landaise

[FOIE GRAS AND CONFIT OF CHICKEN SALAD]

1 POUND CHICKEN GIBLETS (HEART AND GIZZARDS ONLY)

3 TABLESPOONS COARSE SALT

2 POUNDS GOOSE FAT (SEE NOTE)

1 TABLESPOON RED WINE VINEGAR

3 TABLESPOONS OLIVE OIL

4 CUPS MIXED SALAD GREENS, SUCH AS LEAF LETTUCE, ROMAINE, ESCAROLE, AND RADICCHIO

4 TO 6 OUNCES FOIE GRAS, SLICED THIN (SEE NOTE)

¼ CUP TOASTED WALNUTS, FINELY CHOPPED

Trim the giblets of all connective tissue and cut in ½-inch pieces. Sprinkle the giblets with the salt and place in a covered container. Refrigerate for 6 to 7 hours. Remove and rinse well. Pat the giblets dry with paper towels.

In a skillet, melt the goose fat slowly over very low heat. Add the giblets and cook very slowly, about 1 hour, until tender. (This method of cooking poultry parts in fat makes them succulent.) Drain well. Keep warm.

Whisk together the vinegar and oil. Toss the salad greens with the giblets and the vinaigrette and arrange on 4 plates. In a skillet, quickly brown the foie gras slices. Arrange over the salad. Sprinkle with the walnuts and serve.

SERVES 4

NOTE: See Directory for sources of goose fat and foie gras. The goose fat can be strained and stored in the refrigerator.

Chou Farci à l'Auvergnat

[STUFFED CABBAGE
AUVERGNAT STYLE]

This dish, like so many savory baked and stewed bistro dishes, tastes even better reheated on the day after preparation.

2 MEDIUM ONIONS, QUARTERED
1 SMALL BUNCH PARSLEY
2 GARLIC CLOVES
1 LEAF SWISS CHARD
2 LARGE EGGS
1 POUND SAUSAGE MEAT
½ POUND GROUND VEAL
3 TABLESPOONS ALL-PURPOSE FLOUR
2 TEASPOONS SALT
½ TEASPOON FRESHLY GROUND PEPPER
18 LARGE GREEN CABBAGE LEAVES, BLANCHED IN SALTED BOILING WATER AND DRAINED
12 BACON SLICES, BLANCHED
1 CUP VEAL OR BEEF BROTH, HOT

Preheat the oven to 350°F.

In a food processor, combine the onions, parsley, garlic, and chard until finely chopped, or chop by hand. In a bowl, thoroughly mix the eggs, meats, flour, salt, and pepper. Divide the mixture evenly; pat into 6 rounds.

For each serving overlap 3 cabbage leaves, forming a circle. Place each meat round in the center of the leaves and wrap to enclose the meat. Place the packages, open side down, snugly in a roasting pan. Crisscross the bacon strips on top of each package. Pour on the broth and bake 1½ hours, or until cabbage is tender and the bacon is crisp. Remove the packages to a serving platter; skim the fat off the broth and pour over the cabbage packages.

SERVES 6

Tarte aux Myrtilles

[BLUEBERRY TART]

. . . .

TART PASTRY

1⅔ CUPS ALL-PURPOSE FLOUR
9 TABLESPOONS UNSALTED BUTTER, CHILLED AND CUT INTO SMALL BITS
YOLK OF 1 LARGE EGG
¼ CUP SUGAR
PINCH SALT
⅓ CUP WATER

. . . .

FILLING

2 LARGE EGGS
2 TABLESPOONS ALL-PURPOSE FLOUR
5 TABLESPOONS SUGAR
1 TEASPOON BAKING POWDER
3 CUPS BLUEBERRIES (SEE NOTE)
CONFECTIONERS' SUGAR

TO MAKE THE PASTRY: In a bowl and using your fingers, combine the flour, butter, egg yolk, sugar, and salt for about 15 seconds. Add the water and form the dough into a ball. On a floured pastry board or other work surface, knead the dough for about 1 minute, until the texture is uniform and the dough has body. Wrap in plastic and chill for 1 hour.

Preheat the oven to 375°F.

On a floured pastry board, roll out the crust to line a 10-inch tart pan.

TO MAKE THE FILLING: Beat the eggs, flour, 2 tablespoons of the sugar, and baking powder together until light and creamy. Fold in the blueberries and spoon into the tart shell. Sprinkle with the remaining sugar. Bake for 30 to 45 minutes, until well browned and crusty. Cool completely, and remove the tart pan.

Sprinkle with confectioners' sugar.

SERVES 8 TO 10

NOTE: The European whortleberry (myrtille) is not cultivated in the United States, but the blueberries sold in U.S. supermarkets are very similar and are the ones we used for this recipe. (Myrtilles are available in some specialty groceries; they are much smaller than our blueberries.)

. . . .

TO CAP A COPIOUS MEAL, WHICH MIGHT INCLUDE A SERVING OF TARTE AUX MYRTILLES, BISTRO PATRONS SOMETIMES ENJOY A *DIGESTIF* SUCH AS COGNAC.

WAITERS OF L'AUBERGE PYRÉNÉES-CÉVENNES AWAIT THE ARRIVAL OF THE EVENING'S DINERS AT THE ZINC-TOPPED BAR.

L'AUBERGE PYRÉNÉES-CÉVENNES

[C H E Z   P H I L I P P E]

Deep in the 11th *arrondissement,* a somewhat drab commercial area just beyond the limits of the newly fashionable Marais and Bastille *quartiers,* is the perfect provincial *auberge,* tranquil and timeless. The decor of Chez Philippe would not be out of place —would perhaps be more *in* place—in a small village restaurant in southwest France. With its heavily timbered ceiling, dark woodwork, floors of terra-cotta *tommettes,* and adornments that include a suspended anchor, a stuffed stag's head, and old bullfighting posters, the atmosphere is warm and rustic, almost protective. Combine this setting with excellent, rich bistro fare that favors the cuisines of Burgundy and southwest France, and the result is a singular address in Paris, a place to go to escape a dark and dismal November day and urban cares that know no season.

Philippe Serbource, a big, genial man who inspires confidence in his customers and loyalty in his staff, acquired the long-existing Auberge Pyrénées-Cévennes in the mid-  1960s. Since the *auberge* was a restaurant with a distinctive style and a faithful clientele, Phi- lippe decided to maintain the name, appending his own to it. He freshened the interior, begrimed by years of Gauloise smoke, with a coat of cream- colored paint and added a number of dishes from his native Burgundy to the menu, balancing the many specialties from Toulouse and points west. Otherwise, the Auberge Pyrénées-Cévennes is as it always was.

When Philippe acquired his *auberge*, tram rails still ran down the nearby boulevards, and shops of metalworkers and printers made up the neighborhood. The trams are gone, and attrition has greatly diminished the number of local artisans. But the neighborhood continues to thrive, with the arrival of such newly headquartered businesses as the elite fabric house of Braquenié and other decorating concerns seeking more spacious accommodations for their fashionable enterprises. Chez Philippe thrives as well, constantly receiving good notices from Paris critics and drawing diners from all over town to the long, skinny rue de la Folie-Méricourt.

"It was here," Philippe relates with pride, "that Robert de Niro was fattened up for his role as Jake La Motta in the movie *Raging Bull.*" De Niro's producers could hardly have chosen a better place. The menu weighs in with special-

ties from two of the gastronomically richest regions in France, many dishes featuring duck, goose, foie gras, and thick, winy sauces. For starters, among the many choices, there are satiny pink slices of *foie gras naturel*; Piperade Basquaise (scrambled eggs Basque style, with peppers and tomatoes), which would make a fine light supper on its own; Jambon Persillé (parsleyed ham); and a generous basket of *cochonnailles* (assorted pork sausages), from which the diner serves himself. Preeminent among the main courses is the sumptuous Cassoulet Toulousain (cassoulet Toulouse style), a vision of plenty—goose confit, sausages, meaty chunks of pork, and white beans—served up hot in a gleaming copper casserole. Many months after my last dinner there, I still think with regret of the cassoulet I had to leave unfinished. Other Auberge classics are the savory Coq au Vin (chicken braised in wine), the *côtes de boeuf marchand de vin* (a magnificent slice of beef "wine merchant style," with a rich, deep-brown red-wine sauce), and the *paella valenciana*, the best in Paris. Desserts, for those who believe

they will still be able to rise from their seats afterwards, include a Clafoutis aux Pommes et Pruneaux (apple and prune clafoutis), *profiteroles au chocolat*, and a heady *baba au rhum.*

As in any true bistro, there is great familiarity among the customers, proprietor, and staff Chez Philippe. The quintessential *patron*, Philippe knows most of his clients by name and they, in turn, are on a first-name basis with their waiters and waitresses. The banter among them all is as much a part of the daily fare Chez Philippe as the cassoulet. "Conviviality," says Philippe, "is key to a good bistro. And of course good food, a warm welcome, and a pleasing ambiance are primordial. Beyond that, there must be *une générosité*. You have to be a giver." With these words, Philippe Serbource has precisely defined his bistro and himself.

....

THE AUBERGE HAS AN UNPRETENTIOUS, PROVINCIAL AMBIANCE.

Piperade Basquaise

[SCRAMBLED EGGS BASQUE STYLE]

This rich, piquant dish from France's Southwest is hearty enough to be a brunch main course or a simple supper.

3 TABLESPOONS OLIVE OIL

2 LARGE ONIONS, MINCED

3 GREEN BELL PEPPERS, CORED AND SLICED IN ROUNDS

5 LARGE TOMATOES, QUARTERED

SALT AND FRESHLY GROUND PEPPER

2 GARLIC CLOVES, MINCED

12 LARGE EGGS

½ POUND CHORIZO SAUSAGE, SLICED THIN

6 SLICES PROSCIUTTO

Heat 2 tablespoons of the oil in a large skillet and add the onions, peppers, and tomatoes. Stir and cook over medium heat for 30 minutes. Season with salt and pepper

PIPERADE BASQUAISE IS A PIQUANT
STARTER CHEZ PHILIPPE.

. . . .

and stir in the garlic. Set aside to cool.

Preheat the broiler.

In a large bowl, beat the eggs briefly just to blend and add the sausage. Stir in the vegetable mixture. Heat the remaining oil in a large skillet, add the egg mixture, and scramble. Brown the prosciutto quickly in the broiler.

To serve, place the eggs on a shallow, heated serving platter and top with the prosciutto slices.

SERVES 6

Coq au Vin

[CHICKEN BRAISED IN WINE]

Steamed potatoes are a fine accompaniment to this rich Coq au Vin with its delicious sauce. Start preparations a day ahead.

1 4- TO 5-POUND STEWING
CHICKEN, CUT IN 8 PIECES

8 CUPS DRY RED WINE,
PREFERABLY BURGUNDY

2 LARGE ONIONS, QUARTERED

3 MEDIUM CARROTS, QUARTERED

2 GARLIC CLOVES

1 BOUQUET GARNI (1 SPRIG
EACH OF PARSLEY AND THYME,
1 BAY LEAF, AND 1 CELERY
STALK, TIED IN A SQUARE OF
CHEESECLOTH)

2 TABLESPOONS VEGETABLE OIL

1 3-INCH STRIP SALT PORK
RIND, BLANCHED

7 TABLESPOONS COGNAC

SALT AND FRESHLY GROUND
PEPPER

2 TABLESPOONS CORNSTARCH

2 TABLESPOONS COLD WATER

. . . .

GARNISH

1 POUND SALT PORK, BLANCHED
AND CUT INTO ¼-INCH STRIPS

1 POUND FRESH MUSHROOMS

8 GARLIC CROUTONS (SAUTÉED
ROUNDS OF FRENCH BREAD
RUBBED WITH GARLIC)

Place the chicken, wine, vegetables, garlic, and bouquet garni in a large bowl. Cover and marinate in the refrigerator for 24 hours.

Remove the chicken pieces from the marinade and reserve the marinade. Pat the chicken dry with paper towels. In a casserole heat the oil over medium heat, add the chicken pieces, and brown. Remove the vegetables from the marinade and add to the chicken with the pork rind, once again reserving the marinade, and discarding the bouquet garni. Cover and warm 10 minutes on low heat. Add the cognac and ignite carefully. When the flames subside, season, add the marinade, and simmer for about 2 hours, until the chicken is tender.

Remove the chicken and vegetables from the broth and keep warm. Degrease the sauce and bring the broth to boil. In a small bowl combine the cornstarch with the cold water until smooth and then whisk mixture into the boiling sauce. Reduce over medium heat for 45 minutes, until thickened. Meanwhile, prepare the garnish.

TO PREPARE THE GARNISH: Brown the salt pork strips in a skillet and set them aside with the chicken. Remove all but 2 tablespoons of the

fat from the skillet and brown the mushrooms. Add the mushrooms to the chicken.

To serve, place the reserved chicken, vegetables, and garnish into the sauce to reheat for several minutes. Serve on a large platter with the garlic croutons.

SERVES 8

Poires au Porto

[PEARS IN PORT WINE]

Choose pretty pears with stems for this simple but striking dessert.

6 RIPE, FIRM PEARS

2 CUPS RUBY PORT WINE

½ CUP SUGAR

2 CUPS WATER

Peel the pears, but leave them whole. Core, leaving the stem end intact, and cut off a thin slice at the bottom so that the pears can stand upright. Bring the port, sugar, and water to a boil in a nonreactive

. . . .

FRENCH CHEFS POACH PEARS IN
A VARIETY OF WINES, INCLUDING
RUBY PORT.

saucepan. Place the whole pears in the liquid, lower the heat, and simmer for about 35 minutes, turning the pears occasionally until they are tender. Remove the pears with a slotted spoon and cool.

Reduce the liquid by boiling vigorously for about 10 minutes. Place the pears upright in a serving dish and spoon the syrup over them. Chill before serving.

SERVES 6

Jambon Persillé

[PARSLEYED HAM]

This colorful and easy-to-serve appetizer, which serves twelve, would be a fine addition to an elegant buffet table.

4-POUND SMOKED HAM ON THE BONE

6 MEDIUM CARROTS, PEELED AND SLICED INTO ROUNDS

2 LARGE ONIONS, QUARTERED

2 GARLIC CLOVES, CRUSHED

1 BOUQUET GARNI (1 SPRIG EACH OF PARSLEY AND THYME, 1 BAY LEAF, AND 1 CELERY

· · · · · · · · · · · ·

JAMBON PERSILLÉ IS IMPRESSIVE SERVED EITHER WHOLE OR SLICED.

ALTHOUGH THE NAME OF THE CLASSIC DISH "CASSOULET" DERIVES FROM THE WORD *CASSOLE*, CASSOULET CAN BE COOKED IN ALMOST ANY CASSEROLE.

· · · · · · · · · · · ·

STALK, TIED IN A SQUARE OF CHEESECLOTH)

1 TEASPOON BLACK PEPPERCORNS

2 ENVELOPES UNFLAVORED GELATIN

2 LARGE BUNCHES PARSLEY, LEAVES ONLY

Soak the ham in cold water for 1 hour. Drain.

Place the ham in a large pot, add the carrots, onions, garlic, bouquet garni, and peppercorns and cover with cold water. Cover and simmer for about 1½ hours, until the ham is tender. Cool the ham in the broth.

Remove the ham from the broth. Strain the broth, discarding the solids, and return the broth to the pot. Reduce over high heat to 4 cups. Sprinkle in the gelatin, stirring until dissolved. Place the pot over ice, stirring occasionally until the liquid becomes syrupy.

Cut the ham from the bone into 2-inch strips. In a 9 × 5-inch loaf pan, place the strips in alternate layers with the parsley leaves. Spoon the syrupy broth over the ham loaf and chill until set. Cut a piece of cardboard just large

enough to fit into the loaf pan. Cover with foil, place on top of the loaf, and top with a 2-pound weight. Chill overnight.

To serve, remove the weight and cardboard. Dip the loaf pan briefly in hot water and invert onto a serving platter. Slice with a very sharp knife and serve with a grainy mustard on the side.

SERVES 12

Cassoulet Toulousain

[TOULOUSE-STYLE CASSOULET]

This hearty and sumptuous casserole is time-consuming to create; you should begin some of the preparations a day ahead.

2 POUNDS DRIED WHITE BEANS, SOAKED IN WATER OVERNIGHT

6 OUNCES (1 CAN) TOMATO PASTE

2 BOUQUETS GARNIS (IN EACH, 1 SPRIG OF PARSLEY, 1 SPRIG THYME, 1 BAY LEAF, 1 CELERY STALK, TIED IN A SQUARE OF CHEESECLOTH)

4 TO 6 GARLIC CLOVES, CRUSHED

6 MEDIUM CARROTS

3 MEDIUM ONIONS,
EACH STUDDED WITH
A WHOLE CLOVE

7 OUNCES FRESH PORK RIND,
CUT IN 2 × ½-INCH STRIPS

3 POUNDS PORK SPARE RIBS,
CUT IN 1-RIB SECTIONS

2 TABLESPOONS ALL-PURPOSE
FLOUR

1 BOTTLE DRY WHITE WINE
(ABOUT 3½ CUPS; 750 ML)

SALT AND FRESHLY GROUND
PEPPER

2½ POUNDS TOULOUSE-STYLE
SAUSAGES OR FRESH COARSELY
GROUND PORK SAUSAGES (ABOUT
12 LARGE SAUSAGES)

3 TO 4 PIECES GOOSE CONFIT,
EACH CUT IN HALF; OR ABOUT
4 POUNDS SMOKED GOOSE OR
DUCK CUT IN 8 PIECES; OR
1 SEASONED ROASTED 4- TO
5-POUND DUCK, CUT IN
8 PIECES

1 CUP PLAIN BREAD CRUMBS

Drain the beans. In an 8-quart pot, cover the beans with at least 3 inches water. Stir in the tomato paste. Add 1 of the bouquets garnis, 3 garlic cloves, 3 carrots, 1 onion, and the pork rind.

Bring to a boil, lower the heat, and simmer gently about 1 hour, until beans are tender but still firm. Reserve 3 cups of the cooking liq-

uid if prepared the day before. Drain.

Discard the bouquet garni, garlic, carrots, and onion. Reserve the pork rind. (If preparing a day ahead, refrigerate and moisten with the reserved liquid.)

In a large, deep skillet over medium heat, brown the ribs on all sides in their own fat (in batches, if necessary). Sprinkle with the flour and turn the ribs until the flour is absorbed.

Add the wine and enough water to cover. Add the remaining bouquet garni, carrots, and onions. Bring to a boil, lower the heat, cover, and simmer about 2 hours, until fork tender. Season with salt and pepper. (If preparing a day ahead, cool and refrigerate in the liquid. Skim off some of the congealed fat.)

Prick and brown the sausages in a large skillet. Sprinkle lightly with salt and pepper.

To assemble and bake, bring to room temperature any ingredients prepared the day before. Preheat the oven to 325°F. Rub the side of a very large, high-sided casserole (or a large roasting pan) with

the remaining garlic. Add half of the drained beans. Arrange all of the meats, dispersing them evenly, on the beans. Cover with the remaining beans and the pork rind. Pour on the reserved pork cooking liquid.

Bake 1½ to 2 hours. Each time a crust forms on the cassoulet, press it back into the casserole. Add water (or broth) if the mixture is dry. After 1 hour, sprinkle with crumbs. The cassoulet should emerge bubbling and crusted.

SERVES 12 GENEROUSLY

Clafoutis aux Pommes et Pruneaux

[APPLE AND PRUNE CLAFOUTIS]

This rustic flanlike dessert from the Limousin region of France is wonderful served still warm from the oven accompanied by crème fraîche. Cooled, it makes a nice dessert to take along on a picnic.

1 CUP ALL-PURPOSE FLOUR

¾ CUP SUGAR

PINCH OF SALT

5 LARGE EGGS

2 CUPS MILK

7 TABLESPOONS RUM

12 OUNCES PITTED PRUNES,
HALVED

2 APPLES, PEELED AND THINLY
SLICED

CONFECTIONERS' SUGAR

Preheat the oven to 375°F. Butter a round 10 × 2-inch baking dish.

Mix the flour, sugar, salt, eggs, milk, and rum until smooth. Arrange the prunes and apples in the pan and pour the batter over them.

Bake until puffed and golden brown, about 40 minutes. Sprinkle with confectioners' sugar and bake 5 minutes longer. Let cool to lukewarm and serve cut into wedges.

SERVES 12

RELATED TO A FRUIT COBBLER, THE *CLAFOUTIS CHEZ* PHILIPPE IS PREPARED WITH APPLES AND PRUNES, RATHER THAN WITH THE MORE TRADITIONAL BLACK CHERRIES.

S T R O S

A COLLECTION OF FLEA MARKET FINDS—SOME FOR SALE—IMBUE THE BISTRO D'À CÔTÉ WITH OLD-WORLD ATMOSPHERE.

Terrine de Foie
de Volaille Campagnarde

Gratin de Macaroni à l'Ancienne

Clafoutis Chaud aux Framboises
....
Galette de Pommes de Terre au
Chèvre en Salade

Langue de Veau en Pot-au-Feu

Pots de Crème au Chocolat

LE BISTRO D'À CÔTÉ

When the small, nineteenth-century *épicerie* next door to Michel Rostang's elegant two-star restaurant was put up for sale, the acclaimed chef faced an intriguing problem. "I knew I wanted it," he says, "but I had no idea what to do with it." After acquiring the property, he decided to open another restaurant, but one a world away in style, ambiance, and food from the Restaurant Michel Rostang, which reigns over the corner of the rue Rennequin and the rue Gustave Flaubert in the fashionable, residential 17th *arrondissement*. "I thought I would do a bistro for fun," he explains. "I've always loved the simple, regional food of a classic bistro, as well as the convivial atmosphere and the small, close tables." Conceived and developed in 1986, the Bistro d'à Côté (the Bistro Next Door) was born early the following year and was an instant hit.

So beguiling, so "bistrolike" is the decor it could be a Hollywood set. In fact, Rostang changed little from the *épicerie*'s existing interior. On one side of the restaurant is a wall of marble shelves where the dairy products were displayed long ago. (The enameled letters BOF signifying a *beurre-oeufs-eggs-cheese* shop, remain melded on the window.)

. . . .

On the opposite wall are the ceiling-high wooden shelves and worn cabinets where the dry goods were stocked. Rostang and his wife, Marie-Claude, inveterate collectors who scour the flea market weekly for all manner of culinary collectibles—Barbotine faience tureens, figurative Art Deco pitchers, antique "publicity plates" with company logos and slogans, engravings, early *Michelin* guides—have filled the shelves with their finds. Some of these unique *objets* are even for sale. Old marble bistro tables and wooden chairs, lined up along the walls and windows, fill the little space to its limits. When the bistro is fully booked, as it almost always is, the harried waiters, perpetually in motion, are obliged to snake-dance their way through the tables to serve the steaming fare to diners wedged in at seemingly inaccessible angles. But in the merry and noisy atmosphere that characterizes Rostang's creation, nobody seems to mind the *coude-à-coude*, the elbow-to-elbow accommodations.

A large blackboard suspended from the ceiling displays the daily specials. Rostang, originally from Grenoble, where he started cooking when he was only knee-high to his father, the owner of an inn in the mountainous countryside, has chosen several dishes from his native region, as well as many classic specialties from Lyons. "What I offer at the Bistro d'à Côté is the kind of food I like to prepare at home on a Sunday with friends," says Rostang. Among the daily choices are a warm salad of lentils and *cervelas*, Gratin de Macaroni à l'Ancienne (old-fashioned baked macaroni), a golden-crusted *gras-double* (tripe served with steamed parsleyed potatoes), and Clafoutis Chaud aux Framboises (warm clafoutis with raspberries). In counterpoint to these dishes are more piquant specialties from other regions, such as carpaccio of tuna bathed in extra-virgin olive oil and flecked with fresh basil and *pétoncles à la provençal* (bay scallops sautéed Provençal style with garlic and tomatoes).

Rostang, who still spends most of his time in his *grand-luxe* establishment, drops into his bistro annex every day before lunch and dinner, peering into the simmering pots, glancing at the reservations list, and chatting with the chefs and waiters. The kitchen and staff of the two restaurants are completely separate, but the same premium-quality provisions that are bought for the Restaurant Michel Rostang also stock this bistro. Thrice weekly before dawn, Rostang makes the trek to Rungis, the vast wholesale food market eight miles southeast of Paris. There he, like other top Paris chefs, has his own favorite suppliers, who save their best meat, poultry, and produce for him.

Rostang's bistro venture began as a lark, but rapidly became a dramatically successful enterprise—so successful, in fact, that a second Bistro d'à Côté has opened several blocks away on the avenue de Villiers. A patchwork of authentic details, the Bistro d'à Côté is a nostalgic homage to an old way of dining that has tremendous contemporary appeal.

Terrine de Foie de Volaille Campagnarde

[CHICKEN LIVER PÂTÉ
COUNTRY STYLE]

With this tempting country pâté, Michel Rostang suggests serving pickled cherries and a small green salad—and of course a crusty loaf of peasant bread.

3 POUNDS CHICKEN LIVERS

½ CUP VEGETABLE OIL

1½ POUNDS LEAN, BONELESS PORK SHOULDER, CUBED

½ CUP COGNAC

2 SHALLOTS, CHOPPED

1 TABLESPOON SALT

2 TEASPOONS FRESHLY GROUND PEPPER

1 TEASPOON MINCED GARLIC

1 TEASPOON SUGAR

½ TEASPOON FRESHLY GRATED
NUTMEG

1 CUP PLUS 2 TABLESPOONS
CRÈME FRAÎCHE

3 LARGE EGGS

1¼ POUNDS BACON SLICES,
BLANCHED

Preheat the oven to 325°F.

Trim the livers of dark spots, fat, and connective tissue. Heat the oil in a large skillet and brown the livers over high heat until colored. Do not overcook. Drain the fat from the livers, set aside one-third of them, cover, and refrigerate.

Combine the remaining two-thirds of the livers with the pork shoulder, cognac, and shallots in a bowl. Cover and marinate in the refrigerator at least 6 hours or overnight.

Pass the meat mixture along with its marinade through a fine meat grinder. Add the salt, pepper, garlic, sugar, and nutmeg. Stir in the crème fraîche, and beat in the eggs one at a time until blended.

Arrange the bacon slices across the bottom of a 9 × 5-inch loaf pan so that they overhang the long edges of the pan. (It is not neces-

. . . .

THE PÂTÉ CAN ALSO BE SERVED AS
PARTY HORS D'OEUVRES.

sary to line the ends of the pan.) Add a layer of liver mixture, one-third of the reserved whole livers, then a layer of bacon. Repeat with the remaining ingredients, ending with the meat mixture. Fold the overhanging bacon over the top.

Place the loaf pan in a bain-marie or a larger pan filled with hot water. Bake for about 2 hours, until the juices run clear. Remove from the oven. Invert the pan on a rack over a baking sheet to drain off the liquid. Place a piece of foil-wrapped cardboard over the pâté and put a 2-pound weight on top. Refrigerate overnight.

To serve, remove the weight and foil-wrapped cardboard and invert onto a serving platter.

SERVES 16

Gratin de Macaroni à l'Ancienne

[OLD-FASHIONED BAKED
MACARONI]

½ POUND ELBOW MACARONI

7 OUNCES PROSCIUTTO, CUT IN
STRIPS

3 OUNCES BLANCHED BACON,
CUT IN STRIPS AND BROWNED

1½ CUPS CRÈME FRAÎCHE

1½ CUPS MILK

SALT AND FRESHLY GROUND
PEPPER

2 TABLESPOONS GRATED
PARMESAN CHEESE

1 CUP GRATED GRUYÈRE CHEESE

Preheat the oven to 425°F.

Cook the macaroni in salted boiling water until still quite firm. Drain. Mix the macaroni with the prosciutto, bacon, crème fraîche, and milk, and adjust the seasoning. Spread in a buttered shallow oven-proof glass or earthenware casserole. Sprinkle with the cheeses. Bake for 25 minutes, until the

GRATIN DE MACARONI IS A FAVORITE
GRANDMOTHERLY DISH.

. . . .

cheese is browned on top and the liquid is completely absorbed. Let sit 5 minutes before serving.

SERVES 6

Clafoutis Chaud aux Framboises

[WARM CLAFOUTIS WITH
RASPBERRIES]

8 OUNCES SHELLED ALMONDS

¾ CUP ALL-PURPOSE FLOUR

9 LARGE EGGS, SEPARATED

1⅓ CUPS GRANULATED SUGAR

10 OUNCES (2½ STICKS)
UNSALTED BUTTER, MELTED

1 CUP CONFECTIONERS' SUGAR

2 CUPS FRESH RASPBERRIES

Preheat the oven to 400°F.

Grind the almonds finely with the flour in a food processor or blender. Beat the egg yolks with 1 cup of the sugar until pale and thick. Stir in the melted butter. Fold in the almond flour. Beat the egg whites with the confectioners'

CLAFOUTIS ARE SERVED WARM.

. . . .

sugar until soft peaks form. Fold into the yolk mixture.

Spoon the batter into 6 buttered shallow 6-inch baking dishes and drop about 8 raspberries on the top in each dish. Bake for 18 to 20 minutes, until golden brown.

Puree the remaining berries with the remaining sugar and pour the sauce onto 6 dessert plates. Top each plate with a warm cake.

SERVES 6

Galette de Pommes de Terre au Chèvre en Salade

[WILD GREENS SALAD WITH POTATO CAKE AND WARM GOAT CHEESE]

1 POUND POTATOES, UNPEELED

1½ POUNDS FRESH GOAT CHEESE (CHÈVRE)

SALT AND FRESHLY GROUND WHITE PEPPER

14 TABLESPOONS EXTRA-VIRGIN OLIVE OIL

3 CUPS MIXED WILD SALAD

GREENS (ARUGULA, DANDELION, PURSLANE, AND MÂCHE) (SEE NOTE)

½ CUP BLACK OIL-CURED OLIVES, PITTED AND CHOPPED

Preheat the oven to 350°F.

In a medium pot, cook the potatoes in enough water to cover until tender, about 15 minutes. Drain and peel, then slice thin.

Mash the goat cheese and season with the salt and pepper. Place 1 tablespoon of the olive oil in each of 6 4-inch ramekins or small gratin pans. Using half of the cheese, spread a small circle of cheese in each pan. Top with the potato slices, cover with the remaining cheese, and glaze with a tablespoon of oil.

Bake the ramekins until the cheese is lightly golden, 30 to 40 minutes. Let cool to lukewarm.

To serve, toss the greens with the remaining 2 tablespoons olive oil and season to taste. Divide the greens among 6 plates and place a cake on each plate. Sprinkle each cake with the chopped olives.

SERVES 6

NOTE: In France this mixture of wild greens is called *mesclun*.

Langue de Veau en Pot-au-Feu

[VEAL TONGUE POT-AU-FEU]

. . . .

VEAL

3 POUNDS VEAL TONGUE (ABOUT 2 TONGUES)

4 CUPS VEAL STOCK

1 MEDIUM CARROT, QUARTERED

1 MEDIUM ONION, QUARTERED

1 GARLIC CLOVE, CRUSHED

1 BOUQUET GARNI (1 SPRIG EACH PARSLEY AND THYME AND 1 BAY LEAF, TIED IN A SQUARE OF CHEESECLOTH)

1 TEASPOON BLACK PEPPERCORNS

1 TABLESPOON SALT

. . . .

GARNISH

16 SMALL POTATOES, PEELED

8 SMALL TURNIPS

8 SMALL YOUNG CARROTS

16 SMALL ONIONS

1 POUND ZUCCHINI, CUT IN 2-INCH CHUNKS

. . . .

. . . .

THE BISTRO D'À CÔTÉ OFFERS A VARIATION ON THE TRADITIONAL CHÈVRE SALAD.

MANY MEATS CAN BE COOKED POT-AU-FEU STYLE, INCLUDING VEAL TONGUE.

. . . .

Pots de Crème au Chocolat

[CHOCOLATE POTS DE CRÈME]

2 CUPS MILK

1 CUP SUGAR

½ POUND SEMISWEET CHOCOLATE, BROKEN INTO PIECES

YOLKS OF 8 LARGE EGGS

1 LARGE EGG

Preheat the oven to 350°F.

Bring the milk and sugar to a boil in a medium saucepan. Stir in the chocolate pieces and bring back to a boil, stirring often. Whisk the yolks and the egg together and very gradually whisk in the hot chocolate mixture. Pour into eight ½-cup ramekins, and place the ramekins in a larger pan filled with enough hot water to come halfway up the ramekins. Bake for 20 to 30 minutes, until the chocolate mixture is set. Cool and refrigerate until ready to serve.

SERVES 8

VINAIGRETTE SAUCE

2 TEASPOONS DIJON-STYLE MUSTARD

SALT AND FRESHLY GROUND PEPPER

¼ CUP WHITE WINE VINEGAR

⅔ CUP OLIVE OIL

⅓ CUP FINELY CHOPPED MIXED FRESH HERBS (PARSLEY, TARRAGON, CHERVIL, AND CHIVES)

TO PREPARE THE VEAL: Trim the fat from the tongues and place in a large pot with the stock, vegetables, garlic, bouquet garni, peppercorns, and salt. Bring to a boil, lower the heat, and simmer 2½ hours, until the tongues are tender. Remove the tongues from the stock and peel off the skin. Strain the stock and discard the vegetables. Slice tongues ¼ inch thick, return to the stock, and keep warm.

TO MAKE THE GARNISH: Place the garnish vegetables, except zucchini, in a steamer and steam until crisp-tender, 8 to 10 minutes. Add the zucchini and steam about 5 minutes longer.

TO MAKE THE VINAIGRETTE: While the vegetables are steaming, prepare the vinaigrette by whisking the mustard, salt, pepper, and vinegar together and gradually beating in the olive oil until creamy. Stir in the herbs.

To serve, place the garnish vegetables on a heated platter with the tongue slices and a bit of the stock. Drizzle the vinaigrette over all. Serve hot.

SERVES 6 TO 8

. . . .

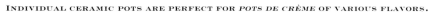

INDIVIDUAL CERAMIC POTS ARE PERFECT FOR *POTS DE CRÈME* OF VARIOUS FLAVORS.

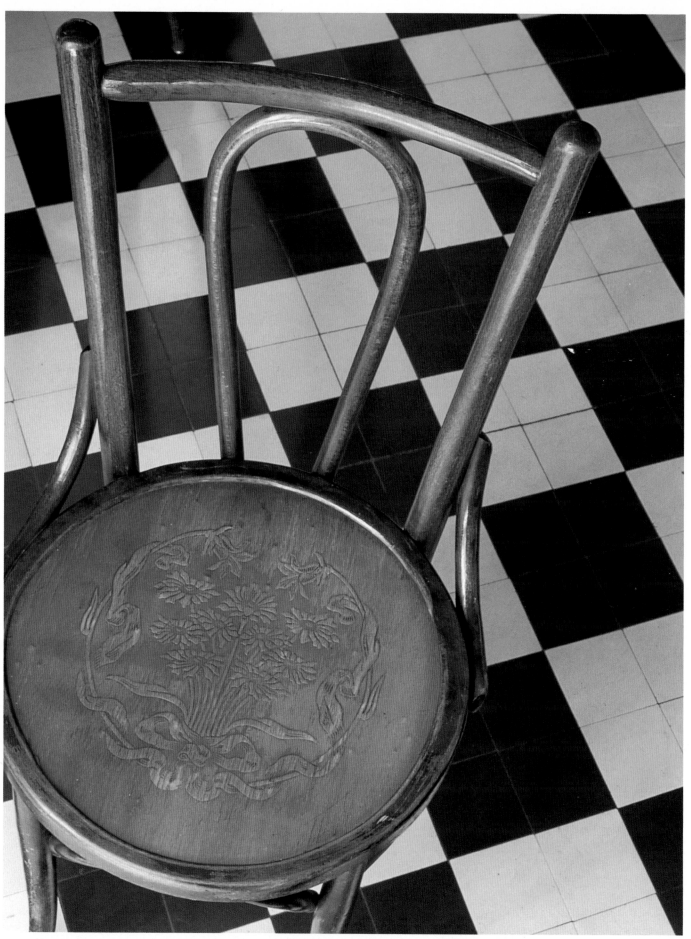

THE BLACK AND WHITE FLOOR TILES OF LA CAFETIÈRE ARE A PROMINENT FEATURE OF THE BISTRO'S HOMEY ATMOSPHERE.

LA CAFETIÈRE

*a*n arresting collection of colorful enameled *cafetières* (coffeepots) —round, octagonal, tall, squat, floral, checked, and spattered— dominates the subdued interior of La Cafetière, a petite and popular bistro on the Left Bank, just off the Boulevard Saint-Germain. La Cafetière's antique *cafetières,* visible through the windows and open doorway, frequently attract attention from passersby on the rue Mazarine. Thus, daily, new clients join artists and owners of the neighboring galleries, editors from Flammarion and other nearby publishing houses, the *immortels* of the Académie Française, and film stars such as Alain Delon and Isabelle Adjani, who have made this appealing spot their own.

La Cafetière has been converting the curious into habitués since 1964, when the restaurant was created by two partners, Jean Romestant, a former theatrical agent, and Louis Diet, a career officer in the merchant marine, from a space once used as a commercial storeroom. At first torn between creating a restaurant that recalled the Vendée region on the Atlantic coast, and one that had a nostalgic, old Paris theme, the partners opted for the latter after Jean Romestant received an imposing antique *cafetière* as a Christmas present several months before the restaurant's opening. "Fate, or rather

SMALL PROPORTIONS AND AN IMPRESSIVE COLLECTION OF *CAFETIÈRES*
(COFFEEPOTS) GIVE THE DINING ROOM ITS INTIMATE APPEAL.

. . . .

Père Noël, decided it was going to be La Cafetière," Romestant recalls, "although at first we were afraid that people might think it was simply a coffeehouse. But we loved the name, and the nostalgic theme we developed around it, and we decided to follow our hearts. After that, and ever since, I've hunted for *cafetières* everywhere, at the flea market, at local fairs and country antique shops." Antique engravings and posters with a "coffee" theme, as well as photographs, framed poems, and sketches by local artists complement the cozy, *sympathique* tone set by the cheerful coffeepots.

La Cafetière's beige and brown menu features classic bistro cooking with a Lyonnaise slant. Top-of-the-line ingredients and exacting preparation result in dishes that are fresh, full of flavor, but free of fancy flourishes. The perfectly seasoned Lentilles aux Echalotes (lentil with shallot salad) is made from the delicate green lentils from le Puy, in the Auvergne, the finest available; the Entrecôte Grillé Béarnaise (grilled rib steaks with béarnaise sauce) is prepared with

long, thin steaks carefully chosen by Romestant for marbleized fat that melts and bathes the meat as it grills; the intense, velvety Mousse au Chocolat (chocolate mousse), served from a big white crock, is made from a combination of milk chocolate and dark chocolate, and served with little butter cookies with messages such as "Avec Amour" and "A Demain." "We don't like fancy mixtures of ingredients," says Romestant, explaining their culinary approach. "We don't even serve cream with the chocolate mousse. We like everything to taste like itself."

As in many small Paris bistros, there are two rooms for dining *chez* La Cafetière, and, as is frequently the case, one is "in" and the other, attractive and airy as it is, is for newcomers and the overflow crowd. Downstairs, beneath the shelves of *cafetières*, is the only room acceptable for habitués, except when they want a very private tête-à-tête. Then the pretty room at the top of the small, winding stairway is preferable, since they will see no one they know.

Messieurs Romestant and Diet,

one an expansive extrovert, the other friendly but with a more reserved manner, have managed to sustain their partnership for more than a quarter of a century by developing an unusual division of labor that resembles nothing so much as joint custody. They split their time in the restaurant fifty-fifty, each working half the month. So, if you dine at La Cafetière during the first two weeks of the month, you will encounter Monsieur Diet; during the last two weeks, Monsieur Romestant. Rarely do the twain meet. They even have their own team of waiters who only work half the month along with their bosses, and clients who prefer to come when one or the other *patron* is on duty. "It's a method of *cohabitation*," says Romestant, "that happens to work for us perfectly." In this unique arrangement, while the faces of the players on the floor change from week to week, the cast of two in the kitchen—chef Patrick Anatole and his assistant—remains constant so that the food is consistently as good as its notices.

. . . .

A COFFEEPOT ADORNS AN ANTIQUE
BENTWOOD COATRACK.

A BISTRO STAPLE, LENTILS ARE SERVED
EN SALADE AT LA CAFETIÈRE.

. . . .

Lentilles aux Échalotes

[LENTIL WITH SHALLOT SALAD]

8 OUNCES (ABOUT 1¼ CUPS)
FRENCH GREEN LENTILS OR
BROWN LENTILS

1 MEDIUM ONION, STUCK WITH A
WHOLE CLOVE

1 MEDIUM CARROT, SLICED IN
¼-INCH ROUNDS

1 BOUQUET GARNI (1 SPRIG
EACH OF PARSLEY AND THYME
AND 1 BAY LEAF, TIED IN A
SQUARE OF CHEESECLOTH)

1 TEASPOON SALT

5 TABLESPOONS PEANUT OIL

3 TABLESPOONS RED WINE
VINEGAR

SALT AND FRESHLY GROUND
BLACK PEPPER

4 MEDIUM SHALLOTS, MINCED
(ABOUT ¼ CUP)

1 BUNCH PARSLEY, CHOPPED
(ABOUT ¼ CUP)

Rinse the lentils with cold water
and pick over. Drain off the water
and place the lentils in a large pot
with the onion, carrot, bouquet
garni, and the 1 teaspoon salt.

Cover with cold water to ¾ inch
above lentils and bring to a boil.

Lower heat and simmer slowly for
35 to 40 minutes, until tender, adding 2 tablespoons of hot water once
or twice if necessary to keep the
lentils from drying out. Drain. Discard the onion and bouquet garni.
Cool to room temperature.

In a bowl, whisk the oil, vinegar,
and salt and pepper until smooth.
Divide the lentils among 4 plates.
Sprinkle with the shallots and
parsley. Spoon 2 tablespoons of
dressing over each serving.

SERVES 4 TO 6

Sole Grenobloise

[FILET OF SOLE WITH
LEMON AND CAPERS]

. . . .

GARNISHES

2 SLICES DAY-OLD WHITE BREAD,
CRUSTS REMOVED, CUT IN ¼-INCH
CUBES AND BROWNED IN 2
TABLESPOONS BUTTER
(CROUTONS)

1 LEMON, PEEL AND PITH
REMOVED, DICED AND SEEDED

2 TABLESPOONS DRAINED CAPERS

3 TABLESPOONS UNSALTED
BUTTER, MELTED AND SEASONED
WITH SALT AND FRESHLY
GROUND PEPPER

1 TABLESPOON CHOPPED FRESH
PARSLEY

. . . .

FISH

4 SOLE FILETS, ABOUT 6 OUNCES
EACH

SALT AND FRESHLY GROUND
BLACK PEPPER

½ CUP ALL-PURPOSE FLOUR

4 TABLESPOONS VEGETABLE OIL

4 TABLESPOONS (½ STICK)
SALTED BUTTER

Assemble the garnishes. Set aside.
TO PREPARE THE FISH: Season the filets with salt and pepper. Dredge
in flour, shaking off excess. In each
of 2 medium skillets, heat 2 tablespoons of the oil and 2 tablespoons
of the butter over medium-high
heat. Add the filets, lower heat
slightly, and sauté for 4 to 5 minutes on each side, until cooked
through and golden.

Lift each filet (with 2 spatulas, if
necessary) onto a warmed dinner
plate. Garnish each filet with the
croutons, lemon, and capers.
Sprinkle with butter and parsley.

SERVES 4

. . . .

AS IN MANY PARIS RESTAURANTS, SOLE IS FILLETED AT THE TABLE BY THE WAITER.

OLD ENAMELED COFFEEPOTS ARE THE SIGNATURE DECORATION OF LA CAFETIÈRE.

Mousse au Chocolat

[CHOCOLATE MOUSSE]

8 OUNCES SEMISWEET OR BITTERSWEET CHOCOLATE, CUT IN SMALL PIECES

5 TABLESPOONS WATER

2 TABLESPOONS UNSALTED BUTTER, AT ROOM TEMPERATURE

1 TABLESPOON CRÈME FRAÎCHE OR SOUR CREAM, AT ROOM TEMPERATURE

5 LARGE EGGS, SEPARATED, AT ROOM TEMPERATURE

PINCH SALT

1 TABLESPOON SUGAR

For best results, all ingredients should be at room temperature.

In a heavy medium saucepan over low heat, melt the chocolate with the water, stirring until smooth and shiny. (The mixture must never be hot, only warm to the touch.) Remove from the heat. Stir in the butter and crème fraîche slowly until smooth. Whisk in each yolk, one at a time, gently and

. . . .

THE RICH, INTENSE MOUSSE AU CHOCOLAT IS PREPARED FAMILY-STYLE.

slowly so as not to stiffen the chocolate, but still to maintain the gloss.

In the bowl of an electric mixer beat the whites with the salt until foamy. Add the sugar and beat until stiff but not dry. Scrape the chocolate mixture into a medium bowl.

Stir a small amount of the whites into the chocolate. Fold in the remaining whites until almost smooth (small bits of egg white may remain).

Scrape into a serving bowl; cover loosely and refrigerate, preferably overnight. Mousse is best chilled 24 hours.

SERVES 6

Tarte aux Poireaux

[LEEK TART]

. . . .

PASTRY

1 CUP PLUS 2 TABLESPOONS ALL-PURPOSE FLOUR

7 TABLESPOONS UNSALTED BUTTER, SOFTENED

PINCH SALT

3 TO 4 TABLESPOONS WATER

. . . .

FILLING

2 POUNDS LEEKS, YOUNG AND SMALL

6 TABLESPOONS (¾ STICK) UNSALTED BUTTER

2 LARGE EGGS

10 TABLESPOONS CRÈME FRAÎCHE

SALT AND FRESHLY GROUND BLACK PEPPER

GRATED NUTMEG

TO MAKE THE PASTRY: In a bowl, using fingertips, mix the flour, softened butter, and the salt, adding just enough of the water to form a ball. Do not overwork the mixture.

TARTE AUX POIREAUX BEGINS WITH LEEKS FRESH FROM THE MARKET.

. . . .

Cover and chill for several hours.

TO MAKE THE FILLING: Trim and discard the root ends and green tops of the leeks. Halve each leek lengthwise. Cut crosswise in 1½-inch lengths. Rinse well to remove any sand. Drain.

In a large skillet, heat the butter. Stir in the leeks. Cover and cook over low heat, stirring occasionally, for about 15 minutes, until tender.

In a medium bowl whisk the eggs and crème fraîche. Season lightly with salt, pepper, and grated nutmeg.

Preheat the oven to 375°F. Roll the chilled dough on a lightly floured surface into a 12-inch circle. Pat into a 10-inch tart pan so that the dough extends up over the edge by ¼ inch. Prick the bottom and sides with a fork and gently line with a sheet of foil, pressing against the bottom and sides. Bake for 6 minutes. Remove the foil. Bake for another 5 minutes, pressing down any pockets with a fork. Spoon on the leeks and pour in the egg mixture. Bake for 30 minutes, or until puffed and golden.

SERVES 4 TO 6

Entrecôte Grillé Béarnaise

[GRILLED RIB STEAK
WITH
BÉARNAISE SAUCE]

Making béarnaise, one of the world's great sauces, requires great care and attention during the preparation; too hot, it will break and lose its thick consistency. Follow the directions carefully and set aside in a warm place while grilling the steaks.

. . . .

BÉARNAISE SAUCE

3 TABLESPOONS WHITE WINE
VINEGAR

3 TABLESPOONS DRY WHITE
WINE

2 TABLESPOONS CHOPPED FRESH
TARRAGON, OR 1 TEASPOON
DRIED

2 TABLESPOONS CHOPPED FRESH
CHERVIL, OR 1 TEASPOON DRIED

2 MEDIUM SHALLOTS, FINELY
CHOPPED

SALT AND FRESHLY GROUND
PEPPER

YOLKS OF 3 LARGE EGGS

10 TABLESPOONS CHILLED
UNSALTED BUTTER

. . . .

RIB STEAK

2 BONELESS RIB STEAKS, ABOUT
1¼ POUNDS EACH (ABOUT
1½ INCHES THICK)

2 TABLESPOONS
PEANUT OIL

TO MAKE THE BÉARNAISE: In a small saucepan, bring to a boil the vinegar, wine, 1 tablespoon of the tarragon, 1 tablespoon of the chervil, the shallots, and a pinch of salt and pepper.

Lower the heat and simmer until reduced to 2 tablespoons. Pressing the herbs with the back of a spoon against the pan, strain the liquid into a heavy saucepan.

Carefully whisk in the yolks over very low heat, moving the pan on and off the burner until the mix-

ture thickens. Do not let cook.

Whisk in the butter piece by piece on and off the heat until the sauce thickens and no lumps remain. The sauce should be warm and thick.

Season with salt and pepper, the remaining tarragon and chervil, and a drop of vinegar, if desired.

Prepare the grill or preheat the broiler.

TO PREPARE THE STEAK: Rub the steaks on all sides with the peanut oil. Grill or broil steaks for about 5 minutes on each side for rare, or to desired degree of doneness. Season the steaks with salt and pepper. Cut crosswise in thick slices. Serve with Béarnaise Sauce and *frites* (French fries).

SERVES 4 GENEROUSLY

Oeufs à la Neige

[FLOATING ISLAND]

5 LARGE EGGS, SEPARATED

1 CUP SUGAR

2 CUPS MILK

2 VANILLA BEANS

4 CUPS WATER

PINCH SALT

JUICE OF 1 LEMON

In a medium bowl beat the yolks with 6 tablespoons of the sugar until pale and thick. In a medium saucepan scald the milk with 1 of the vanilla beans. Discard the vanilla bean, and then beat the milk very gradually into the egg mixture. Return the mixture to the pan and cook, stirring constantly with a wooden spoon, for about 10 minutes, until the custard thickens enough to coat the back of the spoon. (Be careful not to let the mixture boil or the eggs will cur-

dle.) Place the pan over ice and stir occasionally to prevent a skin from forming.

While the custard is cooling, beat the whites with the salt and 4 tablespoons of the sugar until stiff peaks are formed.

In a 12-inch skillet, bring the water to a boil with the remaining vanilla bean and the lemon juice. Lower the heat. Using a large kitchen spoon, carefully slide 8 scoops of meringue, one scoop at a time, into the simmering water. Poach the meringue for 1½ minutes, then turn over and poach for 2 minutes longer. Remove the meringues with a slotted spoon to a clean kitchen towel and let cool.

To assemble the dessert, pour the custard in a large serving bowl and float the meringues on top. Combine the remaining sugar with 1 tablespoon of water in a small saucepan and cook over medium heat until golden. Stir in 1 teaspoon of water, which will thicken the mixture. Immediately drizzle the caramel over the meringues and serve.

SERVES 8

. . . .

OEUFS À LA NEIGE IS ALSO CALLED
ÎLE FLOTTANTE.

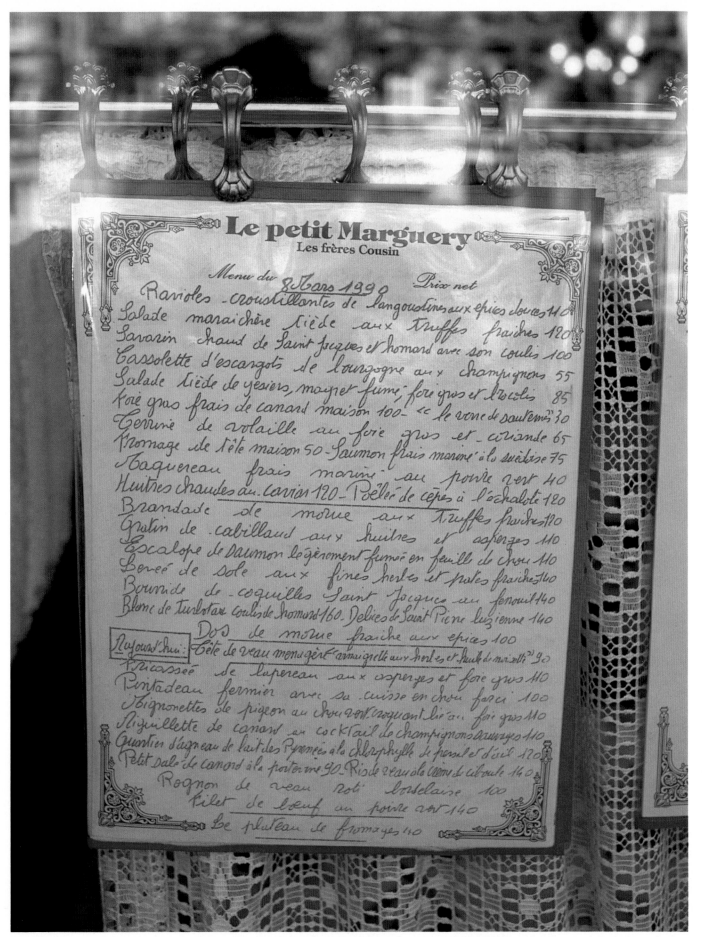

LE PETIT MARGUÉRY OFFERS ITS DAILY MENU TO PASSERSBY.

Salade Maraîchère aux
Truffes Fraîches

Canard au Chou Croquant

Crème Brulée à la Cassonade

. . . .

Maquereau Frais au Poivre Vert

Navarin d'Agneau Printanier

Soupe de Fraises aux Trois Oranges

LE PETIT MARGUÉRY

There is a glow about Le Petit Marguéry that envelops a diner the moment he or she crosses the threshold from the sober Boulevard Port-Royal into the beguiling world of the *frères* Cousin. The glow emanates as much from the sun-washed, Beaujolais-flushed complexions of the chic diners as it does from the terra-cotta—toned walls and the frosted glass lampshades. Jacques, Michel, and Alain Cousin have created, from a classic, turn-of-the-century neighborhood café, a stylish and fashionable eatery very much *à l'air du temps* (of the moment) that draws Parisians from every corner of the city.

Le Petit Marguéry has a contemporary vitality, *joie de vivre*, and freshness, but at heart is a solid *esprit de bistro*, a respect and love for the bistro tradition that keeps the Cousins' operation from being a self-conscious and trendy flash in the pan. "The idea of having a bistro-style restaurant appealed to us," says Michel, who, along with his brother Jacques, commands the kitchen, while brother Alain mans the  front room and the bar. "The cooking is hearty, the ambiance is relaxed and welcoming. It's a place where you can lean back in your chair and celebrate with your friends, a place *pour* *faire la fête*." Before taking over and reincarnat- ing Le Petit Marguéry,

THE THREE COUSIN BROTHERS, CENTER, STAND SURROUNDED BY THEIR KITCHEN AND
SERVING STAFF OUTSIDE THEIR BISTRO ON THE BOULEVARD PORT-ROYAL.

. . . .

Alain, Michel, and Jacques were variously employed at the restaurants L'Archestrate, Michel Guérard's Les Près d'Eugénie, L'Escargot Montorgueil, and the hotels George V and Royal Monceau. They finally pooled their resources and their expertise in the mid-1980s.

Jacques and Michel have created a menu, handwritten and mimeographed, that is grounded in bistro tradition but that puts a personal spin on some classic fare and includes several dishes in a lighter and more sophisticated mode, inspired, says Jacques, "by the beautiful products we find in the market." Old-time classics that appear often, according to the season, include Navarin d'Agneau Printanier (ragout of lamb with spring vegetables), a *tête de veau ménagère* (head-cheese housewife style), Maquereau Frais au Poivre Vert (marinated mackerel with green peppercorns), and a perfect cassoulet. In counterpoint to the classics are dishes such as the *raie rôtie au gingembre et à la menthe* (roast skate with ginger and fresh mint), *escalope de saumon légère-*

ment fumée en feuille de choux (lightly smoked salmon filet enveloped in a bright green cabbage leaf), and Soupe de Fraises aux Trois Oranges, plump, juicy strawberries with three orange accompaniments: sorbet, sliced oranges, and strips of orange zest.

The setting *chez les frères* Cousin is as dynamic and appealing as the cuisine. The Cousins left the fin-de-siècle interior unchanged but revivified the walls, wainscoting, molding, and mirror casements in a playful mix of celadon, terracotta, madder, and sky blue. In contrast to the banquettes and chairs covered in deep red velour, the tables are draped in crisp white linens; the white porcelain tableware is bordered with nasturtiums that echo the colors in Alain's bar bouquet.

Knowing Le Petit Marguéry today, it is hard to imagine that it was once, in the early years of this century, the "local" for a cavalry regiment quartered nearby. Stables behind the premises provided for the officers' horses, while their masters enjoyed a simple supper and Beaujolais from a cask. What

must have been a voluble camaraderie among the young horsemen has been replaced by sophisticated chatter among nattily dressed professionals, and the equine transportation has been superseded by BMWs and Mercedes. But despite the changes—cuisine, clientele, colors, Cousins—for its habitués and its three lively proprietors, Le Petit Marguéry is no less a bistro now than it was then.

Salade Maraîchère aux Truffes Fraîches

[WARM GARDEN SALAD WITH FRESH TRUFFLES]

4 SMALL BROCCOLI FLORETS

8 ASPARAGUS TIPS

4 SMALL LEEKS

1 SMALL RUTABAGA, CUT IN THIN STRIPS

1½ OUNCES TRUFFLES (SEE NOTE), MARINATED FOR 3 DAYS IN ½ CUP PEANUT OIL

2 TABLESPOONS SHERRY VINEGAR

SALT AND FRESHLY GROUND PEPPER

4 CUPS ASSORTED SALAD GREENS, SUCH AS ENDIVE, RADICCHIO, LEAF LETTUCE, ROMAINE, AND ESCAROLE

Blanch the broccoli, asparagus, leeks, and rutabaga in boiling water for 1 minute and set aside, keeping warm.

Make a vinaigrette with the oil from the truffles, vinegar, salt, and pepper. Cut the truffles into thin strips. Place the salad greens on 4 individual plates. Divide the vegetables and arrange on the salad. Strew with the truffle strips and moisten with the vinaigrette.

SERVES 4

NOTE: Truffles are difficult to find in the United States. A good substitute would be fresh shiitake mushrooms. See Directory for sources.

FOR THE SALADE MARAÎCHÈRE, FRESH VEGETABLES ARE BLANCHED JUST BEFORE SERVING.

THE CRISP TEXTURE OF SAVOY CABBAGE IS A PLEASING FOIL TO ROAST DUCK.

. . . .

Canard au Chou Croquant

[DUCK WITH CRUNCHY CABBAGE]

2 4-POUND DUCKS

SALT AND FRESHLY GROUND PEPPER

1 SMALL ONION, SLICED

1 MEDIUM CARROT, CHOPPED

2 SHALLOTS, MINCED

1 GARLIC CLOVE, CRUSHED

4 CUPS SAVOY CABBAGE, CORED AND SHREDDED

1 TABLESPOON COGNAC OR BRANDY

½ POUND RAW FOIE GRAS (THE SPECIALLY LARDED LIVER FROM A FORCE-FED DUCK), DICED (SEE DIRECTORY FOR SOURCES)

Remove the giblets and neck from the ducks. Cut off the wings and backbone and flatten the ducks. Remove as much fat as possible. Lay the ducks skin side up in a large roasting pan and sprinkle with salt and pepper. Refrigerate.

Make a duck stock by placing the giblets, neck, wings, backs, onion, carrot, shallots, and garlic in a medium pot. Cover with water and simmer 1 hour. Strain, discard solids, and degrease stock. Reduce to 1 cup over high heat.

Preheat the oven to 475°F.

Blanch the cabbage for 1 minute in salted, boiling water. Drain. Refresh in cold water, and drain again. Set aside.

Roast the ducks about 12 minutes. Remove from the oven. Pour off the fat. Detach the thigh quarters from the breasts. Cover the breasts to keep warm. Brown the thigh quarters in a medium skillet over medium-high heat for about 2 to 3 minutes on each side.

Deglaze the roasting pan with the cognac mixed with 2 tablespoons of the stock. Scrape the brown bits from the bottom of the pan. Add the remaining stock and reduce by half.

Sauté the duck liver over medium heat for 2 minutes, stirring often. Add the cabbage, correct the seasoning, and heat through. Place the cabbage and foie gras on a heated serving platter. Slice the breasts across the grain and arrange over the cabbage. Place the legs in the center. Moisten the breasts with the stock and serve.

SERVES 4

Crème Brulée à la Cassonade

[CUSTARD WITH BROWN SUGAR GLAZE]

The grains of vanilla bean flecked through the custard make this dessert truly luscious. To gild the lily, the Cousin brothers offer an optional scoop of vanilla or honey ice cream atop the crackling sugar crust.

2 CUPS MILK

2 CUPS HEAVY CREAM

2 VANILLA BEANS, SPLIT

YOLKS OF 7 LARGE EGGS

2 LARGE EGGS

1 CUP GRANULATED SUGAR

⅓ CUP PACKED DARK BROWN SUGAR

Preheat the oven to 300°F.

Combine the milk and cream and scald with the vanilla beans over medium heat. Discard the vanilla beans. In a medium bowl, beat the egg yolks and eggs with the granulated sugar. Gradually beat in the milk. Strain the mixture into a 1½-quart shallow ovenproof dish.

Place the dish in a larger pan of very hot water. Bake until the custard is firm. Let cool.

Just before serving, preheat the broiler and sprinkle the custard with brown sugar. Run the dish under the broiler to caramelize the sugar. Watch carefully to prevent burning.

SERVES 4

Maquereau Frais au Poivre Vert

[MARINATED MACKEREL WITH GREEN PEPPERCORNS]

This cevichelike recipe is an excellent way to prepare an often-overlooked but very flavorful fish. The pastis, an anise-flavored liqueur, offers an unusual zest to the dish.

4 FRESH MACKEREL FILETS

JUICE OF 1 LEMON

1 TEASPOON SALT

½ TEASPOON CRUSHED GREEN PEPPERCORNS

4 TABLESPOONS FINELY CHOPPED MIXED HERBS, SUCH AS PARSLEY, TARRAGON, CHIVES, AND CHERVIL

1 SHALLOT, CHOPPED

½ CUP OLIVE OIL

3 DASHES PASTIS

Slice the fish against the grain, paper thin, with a very sharp, thin-bladed knife.

Combine the remaining ingredients in a small bowl. Place the mackerel on a serving dish and pour the sauce over the mackerel, making sure all slices are covered. Marinate for 1 hour. Serve on a bed of lettuce.

SERVES 4

Navarin d'Agneau Printanier

[RAGOUT OF LAMB

WITH

SPRING VEGETABLES]

· · · · · · · · · ·

LAMB

2 POUNDS BONELESS LAMB SHOULDER, CUT IN 12 PIECES

SALT AND FRESHLY GROUND PEPPER

2 TABLESPOONS PEANUT OIL

2 MEDIUM ONIONS, DICED

2 MEDIUM CARROTS, DICED

2 GARLIC CLOVES, CRUSHED

1 TABLESPOON ALL-PURPOSE FLOUR

2 CUPS WATER

2 MEDIUM TOMATOES, CRUSHED

1 BOUQUET GARNI (1 SPRIG EACH OF PARSLEY AND THYME AND 1 BAY LEAF, TIED IN A SQUARE OF CHEESECLOTH)

· · · · · · · · · ·

GARNISH

4 SMALL TURNIPS

4 BABY CARROTS

4 SMALL ONIONS

8 SNOW PEA PODS

8 SMALL POTATOES, PEELED

TO PREPARE THE LAMB: Season the lamb with salt and pepper. Heat the oil in a large heavy-bottomed casserole and brown the lamb over medium-high heat on all sides. Add the onions, carrots, and garlic. Sprinkle the lamb with the flour and stir until the flour is golden. Stir in the water and add the tomatoes and bouquet garni. Skim off any fat. Correct the seasonings. Cook slowly for 40 to 45 minutes, until the lamb is tender. Remove the lamb from the sauce and set aside, keeping warm. Correct the seasoning.

TO PREPARE THE GARNISH: Separately blanch or steam the garnish vegetables until tender but still crisp. Add the vegetables to the sauce and heat until warm.

Place the lamb on a serving dish, spoon the vegetables on and around the lamb, pour the remaining sauce over the ragout, and serve.

SERVES 4

Soupe de Fraises aux Trois Oranges

[MARINATED STRAWBERRIES

WITH

THREE ORANGES]

ZEST OF 1 ORANGE, CUT IN STRIPS

⅓ CUP SUGAR

3 TABLESPOONS WATER

JUICE OF 1 ORANGE

SOUPE DE FRAISES AND AN ENORMOUS BOUQUET ADORN THE PETIT MARGUÉRY BAR.

· · · · · · · · · ·

2 TABLESPOONS ORANGE FLOWER WATER OR ORANGE-FLAVORED LIQUEUR, SUCH AS TRIPLE SEC, COINTREAU, OR GRAND MARNIER

4 ORANGES, PEELED AND SECTIONED

1½ POUNDS STRAWBERRIES, CLEANED AND HALVED

4 SCOOPS ORANGE SORBET OR SHERBET

4 MINT LEAVES

Blanch the orange zest in boiling water for 2 minutes. Drain, refresh in cool water, and drain again. Combine the sugar and the water in a small saucepan and cook over medium heat until syrupy. Stir once very gently to make sure sugar melts evenly. Add the orange zest, lower the heat, and continue cooking slowly for 6 to 8 minutes, until the zest looks translucent. Stir in the orange juice and orange flower water or liqueur.

Add the orange sections and strawberries and marinate for 1 hour. Divide the fruit among 4 dessert dishes, spoon the juice over them, and top each with a scoop of sorbet and a mint leaf.

SERVES 4

BISTROS

La Poule au Pot

. . . .

Au Chien Qui Fume

. . . .

La Tour de Montlhéry

SET FOR DINNER WITH WINE AND A CHICKEN IN A POT, A TABLE AT LA POULE AU POT OFFERS HEARTY FOOD AND CAMARADERIE.

LA POULE AU POT

The 1930s, a stylish decade of innovative design, have left their distinctive mark on La Poule au Pot, an animated all-night bistro with a *livre d'or* that reads like *Billboard* magazine. Light flows upward from period *torchères* near the entrance; the curved bar topped with a handsome copper *comptoir* is detailed below in an Art Deco design in black marble and honey-toned *faux-marbre;* and ambered-gold columns reflect the light in a thousand tiny mosaic squares. La Poule au Pot, on the rue Vauvilliers just off Les Halles' Place Baltard, was the creation of Madame Suzanne Peniquet who, with her husband, opened her little restaurant in the early 1930s. Madame Suzanne, as everyone knew her, ran her establishment with tremendous pride and courage, particularly during World War II. These two qualities helped her keep her copper bar when most bistros were forced to relinquish theirs to the German Army. When, inevitably, German soldiers arrived to remove the *comptoir,* Madame Suzanne, then a beautiful blonde woman in her mid-forties, opened wide her blue eyes and pleaded, "My bar is everything to my business. I worked so long to have it, and if you take it you will ruin me." Swayed by her words, her plight, and by her charm, the commanding officer spared Suzanne's bar.

After her husband died following the war, Madame Suzanne continued on alone, managing her bistro for three more decades before at last selling it in 1982 to Paul Racat, an ambitious young restaurateur with a genial manner. "Suzanne sold me her restaurant only after extracting a promise from me that I would change nothing until after she died," Racat recalls. "It was a promise I willingly made because I loved the way it was." Suzanne, now almost one hundred years old, still lives just a hundred yards away from her former bistro and is an occasional and beloved presence at a table near the bar.

One of eleven children, Paul Racat followed his two older brothers, who became chefs, into the restaurant business. "We all probably entered the world of professional cuisine in revenge for our childhood experiences with food," he relates. "Our mother was, shall we say, one of the least talented cooks in France. It was like a punishment to sit down at her table." No one loves traditional cooking

. . . .

EVEN THE POSTERS IN LA POULE AU POT'S WINDOWS EVOKE A PREWAR AMBIANCE.

these days more than Racat.

The handwritten menu at La Poule au Pot is simple and straightforward. "I wanted to serve the same kind of home cooking that Suzanne had always served," says Racat. To start there's the onion soup *gratinée*, stuffed mussels, escargots, baked eggs in cream, smoked salmon and several salads, including the *crottin de chèvre chaud sur toast et salade* (warmed goat cheese on toast rounds with green salad), and the Salade "Poule au Pot" (spinach salad tossed with hot sautéed chicken livers and vinegar). Among the main courses is an *escalope de saumon à l'oseille* (salmon filet in a velvety sorrel cream sauce), three variations on a steak filet (*tartare, au poivre,* and *à la moelle* [with marrow]), sautéed veal kidneys, and broiled lamb chops. But the featured dish is, of course, Poule au Pot Garnie (poached stuffed chicken in a pot with vegetables). It is Henry IV who is generally credited for originating this dish. Shortly before he was assassinated in 1610 by François Ravaillac, a political foe, he is supposed to have vowed to the duke of Savoy that if God granted him a longer life, every peasant in his kingdom would have *"une poule dans son pot"* every Sunday night. A comforting staple in the culinary repertoire of French grandmothers, Poule au Pot Garnie simmers with a variety of vegetables for several hours. It can be served as two courses, the broth first with noodles or rice, then the chicken accompanied by the vegetables and a slice of stuffing, or, as at La Poule au Pot, all together in a large soup bowl. Dessert choices, limited but appealing, usually include *pruneaux au vin, parfumé au thé* (prunes macerated in white wine and tea) and the Soufflé Glacé au Framboise or the Soufflé Glacé au Grand Marnier.

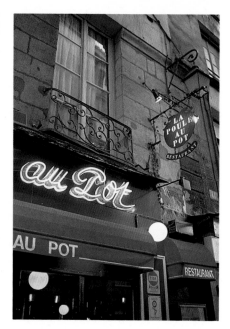

A HANGING POT SIGN IDENTIFIES THE MAIN FARE OF THE LIVELY BISTRO.

. . . .

La Poule au Pot is open from 7 P.M. to 8 A.M. and is dark for the rest of the day. After sunset, as the streetlights blink on, La Poule au Pot comes to life. In the early part of the evening Paul Racat hosts tourists, neighbors, and visitors to Le Forum des Halles and the Centre Beaubourg. After midnight, when the bistro truly blooms, Racat welcomes the entertainers, club crawlers, and insomniacs. His clientele of singers, who arrive voracious after their shows, spans several eras and a wide variety of styles. Names, *bons mots,* and doodles in the *livre d'or* have been inscribed by Frank Sinatra, Joan Baez, Donovan, the Rolling Stones, Bruce Springsteen, Prince, David Bowie, Paul Simon, Santana, and Stan Getz, among many others of many nationalities. Depending on the night, the shows in town, and the hour, the atmosphere at La Poule au Pot can be raucous or eerily calm. With an entourage of rock stars and roadies within, the partying can be heard from the sidewalk; on a Sunday night in June, you can sometimes hear a napkin drop.

Salade "Poule au Pot"

[SPINACH AND SAUTÉED CHICKEN LIVER SALAD]

1 POUND SPINACH, WASHED, DRIED, AND CHOPPED INTO LARGE PIECES

2 TABLESPOONS PEANUT OIL

½ POUND CHICKEN LIVERS, QUARTERED

1 MEDIUM ONION, FINELY MINCED, PREFERABLY IN FOOD PROCESSOR

¼ TEASPOON GROUND WHITE PEPPER

3 TABLESPOONS DRY WHITE WINE

3 TABLESPOONS RED WINE VINEGAR

3 TABLESPOONS THICKENED BEEF OR VEAL STOCK (SEE NOTE)

Put the spinach in a salad bowl and set aside. In a medium skillet, heat the oil over medium-high heat, then add the chicken livers, onion, and pepper. Sauté, stirring frequently with a large spoon, until the livers are browned, about 2 minutes. Stir in the wine, then the vinegar, and finally the thickened stock, mixing to coat the livers well. Lower the heat to medium-low and simmer for 3 more minutes, stirring from time to time.

Remove the pan from heat and spoon the hot livers and sauce over the spinach. Bring to the table, toss, and serve immediately on 4 individual salad plates.

SERVES 4

NOTE: If you do not have fresh beef or veal stock on hand, combine 1 cube or 1 teaspoon beef bouillon powder with 3 tablespoons boiling water in a heatproof cup. To thicken stock, sprinkle with 2 teaspoons flour and then heat, stirring constantly, to desired consistency.

Poule au Pot Garnie

[POACHED STUFFED CHICKEN IN THE POT WITH VEGETABLES]

1 3½- TO 4-POUND CHICKEN

⅓ CUP MINCED ONION

. . . .

PAUL RACAT, WHO GOES THROUGH SCORES OF CHICKENS A WEEK FOR HIS SPECIALTY, MAKES GOOD USE OF THE LEFTOVER CHICKEN LIVERS IN HIS SPINACH SALAD.

1 TABLESPOON MINCED FRESH PARSLEY

¼ POUND GROUND PORK

¼ POUND GROUND VEAL

YOLK OF 1 LARGE EGG

½ TEASPOON SALT

¼ TEASPOON FRESHLY GROUND PEPPER

6 MEDIUM CARROTS, QUARTERED

4 LEEKS, WHITE PARTS ONLY

4 MEDIUM TURNIPS, QUARTERED

1 LARGE ONION, STUDDED WITH 1 WHOLE CLOVE

2 CELERY STALKS, CUT IN 2-INCH LENGTHS

1 BOUQUET GARNI (1 SPRIG EACH OF THYME AND PARSLEY, AND 1 BAY LEAF, TIED IN A SQUARE OF CHEESECLOTH)

8 SMALL POTATOES, PEELED

Clean the chicken, removing all excess fat. Combine the minced onion, the parsley, pork, veal, egg yolk, salt, and pepper in a bowl. Fill the chicken cavity with the mixture and truss the chicken with kitchen string. Place the chicken in a large pot with the remaining ingredients except the potatoes. Add enough cold water to cover. Bring to a boil, cover, and simmer very slowly for 2 hours.

Add the potatoes and simmer 25 minutes longer or until the potatoes are tender. Correct the seasonings. Remove the chicken and vegetables from the stock and keep warm. Degrease the stock. Cut the chicken into serving pieces—wings, legs, thighs—and slice the breast.

Serve all together from a tureen, filling each soup bowl with chicken, a slice of stuffing, vegetables, and broth. Or serve as 2 courses, the broth first, followed by the chicken and sliced stuffing on a platter and surrounded by the vegetables, all moistened with broth (see Note).

SERVES 6

NOTE: Any remaining stock makes great soup or sauce base.

Soufflé Glacé au Framboise

[FROZEN RASPBERRY SOUFFLÉ]

1 QUART FRESH RASPBERRIES

1 CUP PLUS 3 TABLESPOONS
SUGAR

2 TABLESPOONS PLUS
1 TEASPOON WATER

WHITES OF 5 LARGE EGGS

1 CUP CRÈME FRAÎCHE

1 PINT RASPBERRY SORBET

MINT LEAVES

Place the raspberries, 3 tablespoons of the sugar, and 1 teaspoon of the water in a medium saucepan. Bring to a boil, stirring occasionally. Pass through a food mill to remove the seeds, yielding about 1 cup of puree. Set aside.

Place the remaining sugar and 2 tablespoons of water in a small saucepan. Cook over medium-high heat until the syrup reaches 238°F. when measured with a candy ther-

. . . .

THE SOUFFLÉ GLACÉ AU FRAMBOISE IS
AN INDIVIDUAL SERVING.

mometer (soft-ball stage). Beat the egg whites with an electric mixer until soft peaks form. With the speed at medium, very gradually pour the sugar syrup down the side of the bowl. Continue to beat the meringue until it is cool.

Fold ½ cup of the raspberry puree into the meringue. Whip the crème fraîche until soft peaks form and fold into the meringue.

Line 8 4-inch ramekins or bowls with plastic wrap, allowing the edges to hang over the sides. Spoon some of the meringue into each dish. Add a scoop of raspberry sorbet and cover completely with the remaining meringue. Cover each dish with plastic wrap and freeze 2 to 3 hours before serving.

To serve, pour the remaining raspberry puree onto 8 chilled serving dishes. Carefully invert the soufflés onto the plates and remove the plastic wrap. Garnish the soufflés with mint leaves.

SERVES 8

Soufflé Glacé au Grand Marnier

[FROZEN GRAND MARNIER
SOUFFLÉ]

1 CUP SUGAR

7 TABLESPOONS WATER

5 LARGE EGGS, SEPARATED

1½ CUPS CRÈME FRAÎCHE

½ CUP GRAND MARNIER

8 LADYFINGERS

. . . .

ORANGE SAUCE

½ CUP ORANGE MARMALADE

2 TABLESPOONS ORANGE JUICE

2 TABLESPOONS GRAND MARNIER

Place 4 tablespoons of the sugar and 4 tablespoons of the water in a

small saucepan and bring to a boil. In a small bowl break up the egg yolks and gradually whisk in the hot syrup. Set the bowl over a saucepan with hot water for about 2 minutes, stirring constantly until thickened. Be careful not to let the eggs begin to cook, since they will curdle. Set the bowl over ice to cool.

Place the remaining sugar and remaining 3 tablespoons of water in a small saucepan. Cook over medium-high heat until the syrup reaches 238°F. when measured with a candy thermometer (soft-ball stage). Beat the egg whites with an electric mixer until soft peaks form. With machine on medium speed, very gradually pour the sugar syrup down the side of the bowl. Continue to beat the mixture until it is cool.

Beat the crème fraîche until soft peaks form. Fold in ¼ cup of the Grand Marnier. Fold the reserved yolk mixture into the crème fraîche. Then fold the yolk and crème fraîche mixture into the meringue.

Line 8 individual soufflé dishes with plastic wrap, letting the edges hang over the sides. Spoon some meringue mixture into the bottom of each dish. Separate the ladyfingers and brush them with the remaining Grand Marnier. Divide the ladyfingers over the meringue and fill the dishes with the remaining meringue. Cover with plastic wrap and freeze for 2 to 3 hours before serving.

TO MAKE THE ORANGE SAUCE: Liquefy the marmalade in a small pot over low heat. Combine the marmalade with the orange juice and Grand Marnier in a small bowl, stirring to blend the ingredients.

To serve, invert the soufflé dishes onto 8 chilled plates and spoon the Orange Sauce over the top.

SERVES 8

PRUNES POACHED IN RED WINE REST ATOP A PERIOD RADIO AT LA POULE AU POT.

THE SMOKING DOG THEME IS CARRIED OUT EVEN ON THE TABLEWARE.

AU CHIEN QUI FUME

In 1920, the story goes, a new owner took command of the venerable all-night bistro at 33 rue du Pont-Neuf in the heart of Les Halles, bringing with him his two dogs, a Brussels griffon and a poodle, each endowed with an unusual talent. The dogs could smoke. The owner often amused his late-night clientele by having his dogs perform. He placed a lighted cigar between the teeth of the poodle, a lighted pipe between the teeth of the griffon. For several minutes the dogs held the paraphernalia in their muzzles, "smoking." Thus the restaurant acquired the sobriquet Au Chien Qui Fume—At the Smoking Dog.

The smoking dogs were later immortalized in portraits under glass, which were inset into the moldings of the spectacular curved bar, elegantly carved and capped by a shining brass countertop. The bistro's canine theme is carried through with dog tableaux and dog collectibles, many offered by enthusiastic patrons, displayed on walls or in every available niche; a menu decorated with a hound; and two prix fixe menus—the Agathe and the Bazil—after a terrier and a cocker spaniel.

Au Chien Qui Fume, a bustling and cheerful bistro, is open and active until 2 A.M. every day of the year. Popular with the office workers from rue de Rivoli and employees of the Forum des Halles,

THE CLASSIC THREE GRACES WEAR DOG
MASKS AT THIS THEME BISTRO.

. . . .

the vast new commercial complex on the site of the old market district, the bistro, with its prominent corner location, its brightly lit façade and its inviting, unpretentious atmosphere, attracts many tourists strolling through the old Halles area or staying at neighborhood hotels. Habitués and newcomers alike appreciate Au Chien Qui Fume as a place to have an honest, well-prepared meal of traditional French fare that can be ordered, served, eaten, and paid for in the course of an hour. Speed is of the essence among the courteous and efficient serving staff. After midnight, when the pace diminishes, Au Chien hosts the night birds, a species the current owner knows rather well.

Jean-François Llana was a veteran of the late-night scene before he purchased Au Chien Qui Fume in 1980. A native of Nice, Llana came to Paris in 1968 to work with nightclub impresario Jean-Marie Rivière at his newly opened Alcazar and later the Paradis-Latin, clubs noted for their racy revues. Life is tamer now for Llana but

hardly less busy. Almost always present, he oversees every aspect of his enterprise, dashing from the kitchen to a table on the terrace, to the bar, to an upstairs dining room and back to the kitchen, taking orders, making change, even clearing the tables when the waiters are busy with a full house. After acquiring his bistro, Llana set out to reestablish its reputation—sadly diminished during the decade of previous ownership—and its traditional bistro menu.

Among the offerings prepared by Llana's Alsatian chef, Florent Mathis, are a couple of hearty salad starters, such as the *salade du Chien Qui Fume* (spinach and chicken liver salad) and a generous *frisée aux lardons et oeuf poché* (curly endive salad tossed with *lardons* and topped with a poached egg). Also among the appetizers is the classic Gratinée des Halles (classic French onion soup), a deep white bowl of onion soup prepared with white wine and topped with a broiled crust of melted cheese over a *crouton*, or toasted slice of baguette. Even though Llana pronounces the *gratinée* "slightly out of fashion these days," it remains a popular item on the menu, particularly during the winter months. Main courses include bistro perennials like the Lapin à la Moutarde (braised rabbit with mustard sauce), steak tartare, and *pied de porc grillé* (grilled pig's feet) along with a variety of lighter and more contemporary dishes like the appealing *langoustines au beurre d'Aneth* (crayfish in anise butter); and *coquilles Saint-Jacques aux blancs de poireaux au Noilly Prat* (scallops sautéed with the white of a leek and white vermouth). Desserts feature classics such as *île flottante*, *profiteroles au chocolat*, and *tarte tatin*, as well as Fraisier (strawberry génoise) and the *tulipe des fruits frais* (seasonal fruits in a tulip-shaped cookie shell).

The changes in Paris, in Les Halles, and in the establishments on the site of Au Chien Qui Fume have been revolutionary since 1754, when a modest inn opened on the rue du Pont-Neuf facing what was then Les Halles du Roy. Almost a century later, the city planner, Baron Georges Haussmann, whose efforts transformed Paris into a city of *grands boulevards* in the 1850s and 1860s, decided to renovate the area, and the old inn was demolished. Several years later, a new restaurant was created on the site, where the celebrated *forts des Halles*, the robust, ruddy-faced butchers, came for their early morning dinners. Today, for visitors to Le Forum and Pompidou's Centre Beaubourg and neighbors who reside on tiny side streets, Au Chien Qui Fume is the ideal place to dine on a dog-day afternoon, or evening.

Gratinée des Halles

[CLASSIC FRENCH ONION SOUP]

This rich, old-fashioned onion soup is unusual in that it does not have a beef stock base, but instead a base that is a sweet broth created from the sautéed, simmered onions themselves.

4 TABLESPOONS LARD

1 POUND (2 TO 3 MEDIUM) ONIONS, MINCED

1 4 × 4-INCH PIECE BACON RIND, BLANCHED

¼ POUND BACON, DICED AND BLANCHED

2 SPRIGS THYME

2 SPRIGS PARSLEY

1 BAY LEAF

SALT AND FRESHLY GROUND PEPPER

4 CUPS WATER

4 THICK SLICES TOASTED CRUSTY BREAD, PREFERABLY FRENCH

1 CUP GRATED GRUYÈRE CHEESE

4 TEASPOONS UNSALTED BUTTER

Melt the lard in a casserole and stir in the onions, bacon rind, bacon, herbs, and the salt and pepper. Cover and simmer over medium heat for 25 minutes, stirring occasionally. Add water, bring to a boil, lower the heat, and simmer, uncovered, for 1 hour. Discard the bacon rind. Skim off any surface fat from the soup. Correct the seasonings.

Preheat the oven to 450°F.

Place 4 individual ovenproof bowls, about 6 inches across and 3 or 4 inches deep, on a baking sheet. Divide the soup among the bowls and add a piece of toast. Sprinkle the toast heavily with the cheese and dot with the butter. Bake 5 to 10 minutes, until the cheese is melted and the soup is bubbling. Serve immediately.

SERVES 4

Lapin à la Moutarde

[BRAISED RABBIT WITH MUSTARD SAUCE]

With this succulent rabbit dish, Chef Mathis suggests serving fresh buttered pasta.

2 TABLESPOONS LARD

1 2½- TO 3-POUND RABBIT, DRESSED AND CUT INTO 10 SERVING PIECES (EACH BREAST IN TWO, THIGHS, LEGS, AND BACK CUT IN HALF) USING CLEAVER OR BONING KNIFE

SALT AND FRESHLY GROUND PEPPER

4 TABLESPOONS (½ STICK) UNSALTED BUTTER

1 CUP DRY WHITE WINE

1 SPRIG THYME

1 BAY LEAF

½ CUP DIJON-STYLE MUSTARD

5 TABLESPOONS CRÈME FRAÎCHE

Melt the lard in a large skillet over medium-high heat. Brown the rabbit pieces on all sides and season with the salt and pepper. Set the

rabbit aside and discard the lard.

Melt the butter in the skillet and return the rabbit pieces to the skillet. Stir in the wine, herbs, and mustard. Cover and simmer for 20 minutes. Remove the breast pieces, set aside, and keep warm while continuing to cook the leg and thigh pieces 5 to 10 minutes longer. Remove the legs and thighs and set aside with the breasts.

Reduce the sauce by one-third over high heat. Stir in the crème fraîche and correct the seasoning. Serve the rabbit on a platter with the sauce over it.

SERVES 4

Fraisier

[STRAWBERRY GÉNOISE]

GÉNOISE

4 LARGE EGGS

½ CUP SUGAR

1 TEASPOON VANILLA EXTRACT

⅔ CUP ALL-PURPOSE FLOUR

SYRUP

⅓ CUP SUGAR

⅓ CUP WATER

1 TEASPOON VANILLA EXTRACT

FILLING

1 QUART FRESH STRAWBERRIES

2 CUPS HEAVY CREAM

½ CUP SUGAR

1 TEASPOON VANILLA EXTRACT

Preheat the oven to 325°F.

TO MAKE THE GÉNOISE: Beat the eggs, sugar, and vanilla in the bowl of an electric mixer at high speed for 10 to 15 minutes, until very thick and pale. Gradually fold in the flour with a rubber spatula. Grease an 8 × 12-inch baking pan and line the bottom with wax paper. Spread the batter into the pan and bake 30 minutes or until

THE FRAISIER APPEARS AS A SPECIAL DURING THE STRAWBERRY SEASON.

lightly golden. Cool 5 minutes on a rack, loosen the edges of the cake with a knife, and invert onto a rack. Invert onto another rack to finish cooling.

TO MAKE THE SYRUP: Bring the sugar and the water to a boil in a small saucepan. When cool, stir in the vanilla. Set aside.

TO MAKE THE FILLING: Reserve 6 strawberries for the garnish and slice the rest. Whip the cream with the sugar and vanilla until firm.

Assemble the cake: Slice the cake in half horizontally. Place the bottom layer on a serving platter and brush with half the syrup. Spread one-third of the cream on the cake, then a layer of half the strawberries. Cover the strawberries with a layer of one-third of the cream. Top with the remaining layer of cake and brush with the remaining syrup. Cover the top of the cake with the remaining cream. Overlap the strawberry slices around the edge of the cake and garnish with the whole berries. Keep refrigerated until ready to serve. Slice with a very sharp knife.

SERVES 12 TO 16

FRESH SHELLFISH IN ABUNDANCE WELCOMES DINERS TO AU CHIEN QUI FUME.

BEHIND THE BAR, THE ANCIENT CASH REGISTER HAS RUNG UP THE BILLS OF HUNDREDS OF LES HALLES WORKERS.

LA TOUR DE MONTLHÉRY

Deep beneath Paris, particularly beneath the oldest *quartiers* in the center of the City—Les Halles, the Marais, the Ile-de-la-Cité, and the Latin Quarter—lies a subterranean world of tunnels and *caves*—cellars—some dating back to the Middle Ages. Some lead into and out of Notre-Dame, some lead to catacombs, some lead to storage vaults under Les Halles where fruits and vegetables were left to ripen in centuries past, and some lead to the basements of old private homes and restaurants. One vaulted tunnel leads into the medieval *caves,* now used as a wine cellar, of La Tour de Montlhéry, the archetype of the classic Parisian bistro. Lodged in a narrow building in Les Halles, with an early eighteenth-century half-timbered façade and massive, hand-hewn beams within, La Tour de Montlhéry is a boisterous, beloved establishment of red-checked tablecloths, stone walls, aged hams suspended above the bar, blackboard menus, and sawdust-strewn tile floors. In existence for 150 years, the bistro has been run for the last three decades, with an appropriate mix of élan, *bonhomie*, and irreverence, by Jacques and Denise Bénériac. A democratic, "family-of-man" spirit pervades La Tour de Montlhéry, one of the few restaurants in Paris open 24 hours a day. The

portions of *onglet grillé* (grilled hanger steak) or rare *côtes de boeuf* (roast beef). The *haricots de mouton* (casserole of mutton or lamb and white beans) could serve four, as could the *blanquette de veau*. Exceptions to the rule of copious classics are the seafood specials created by Bernard Nöel, a fishing enthusiast during his weekends off. Depending on the day and the season, the blackboard menu might feature delicately piquant Ragoût de Homard (lobster ragout); *brandade de brochet à l'oseille* (baked puree of pike with sorrel), a variation on the traditional *brandade* made with salt cod; *filets de perches aux figues* (perch filets sautéed with fresh figs in a sauce of crème fraîche and raspberry vinegar); or *crêpinettes de carpe aux lentilles* (baked carp dumplings with lentils). The dessert list on the board is short but sweet: *mousse au chocolat, île flottante, crème caramel,* Baba au Rhum, and a daily fruit tart. Choosing a wine is even less taxing than selecting a dessert; only three choices are offered—a Muscadet, a Bordeaux, and a Côtes de Brouilly.

Late one afternoon I found myself deep in the medieval *caves* beneath La Tour de Montlhéry, in the company of Jacques, chef Bernard, and a bottle of Champagne. We had descended through a trap door behind the bar down a narrow ladder. Surrounding us in one vaulted chamber were Jacques's dusty bottles of vintage Bordeaux, his private reserve kept to share with friends. On one shelf I noticed a small human skull, darkened to a deep coffee brown from its several hundred years in an ancient Paris catacomb. An atmospheric touch, I thought, until Jacques took the skull from the shelf and Bernard filled it with Champagne. It was then placed in my hands for the honorary first sip—an old Les Halles tradition, my companions

ancient zinc-topped bar is often crowded with laborers in their worker blues having a glass of Beaujolais alongside white-collar executives extending their long lunch hours with a second cognac. Long tables in the rear, sometimes shared by two or three parties, are claimed by old family friends, neighborhood habitués, singers ("Serge Lamas wrote half his songs on my tablecloths," says Jacques), local artists, and tourists from everywhere on the globe. Young children, old couples— every age and every life-style—are in evidence *chez* Denise, as the restaurant is called by its regulars. During the years when Les Halles still flourished, La Tour de Montlhéry catered almost exclusively to market workers. It was open only from 1 A.M. to 6 A.M., when it was thronged with farmers, truckers, and the famous *forts des Halles*. The little street running past the bistro, the rue des Prouvaires, was part of the vegetable and fruit market, and was jammed with crates, carts, and vendors all night long. Although this lively, noisy era is only a memory, a large wholesale

meat market remains nearby, a holdout against the exodus to Rungis. In the old days, the ruddy-faced and white-coated butchers would come with their own pieces of meat, called *gobots* in argot, to be cooked for them. Now the two dozen or so local butchers, whose names are permanently recorded on a large wall placque in the restaurant, order off the menu when they arrive for dinner at 6 A.M.

Two chefs direct the Bénériacs' large, modern stainless steel and tile kitchen: Bernard Noël, a veteran of sixteen years, during the day, and at night Michel Anfray, in residence for nineteen years. In keeping with the decor and the ambiance, most of the dishes are traditional. Appetizers include *escargots, pâté de campagne, salade frisée* with garlicky croutons of Poîlane bread, *poireaux vinaigrette,* generous charcuterie plates, pork rillettes, and a meal-in-itself, Oeufs en Gelée au Porto (eggs and ham in jellied beef and port consommé). Main courses here are copious, bordering on the gargantuan. The word "slab" hardly serves to describe the daunting assured me. We subsequently shared the rest of the bottle (poured into traditional flutes) and talked of things mortal and immortal, Jacques revealing in the course of the conversation his plan for his own ideal funeral. "There will be some good Auvergnat jazz," he said, "a lot of Côtes de Brouilly for my friends, and I will disappear in the smoke." For this generous, jovial, and unpretentious man, who personifies the true bistro *esprit*, it would indeed be a fitting farewell. At the end of our interlude in the *cave*'s otherworldly ambiance, we toasted *"à la vie, l'amour, la mort"* with one last glass of Champagne, then ascended to the daylight.

Oeufs en Gelée au Porto

[EGGS AND HAM IN JELLIED
BEEF AND PORT CONSOMMÉ]

At La Tour de Montlhéry, these jellied eggs are prepared in pretty white oval porcelain molds.

. . . .

SAVORY OEUFS EN GELÉE AU PORTO ARE
ALMOST A MEAL IN THEMSELVES.

4 CUPS WATER

2 TABLESPOONS WHITE WINE
VINEGAR

6 LARGE EGGS

1½ CUPS BEEF STOCK

1 ENVELOPE UNFLAVORED
GELATIN

½ CUP PORT WINE

2 MEDIUM TOMATOES, CUT INTO
6 SLICES

6 OUNCES CURED (BAYONNE)
HAM, CUT IN FINE STRIPS

6 SMALL SPRIGS CHERVIL OR
TARRAGON

Bring the water and the vinegar to simmering and poach the eggs for 4 minutes. With a slotted spoon remove the eggs to a kitchen towel and let cool.

In a medium saucepan, bring the beef stock to a boil. Soften the gelatin in the wine and stir into the stock. Remove from the heat, pour the stock into a bowl, and set the bowl over ice. Stir occasionally until syrupy.

Place the tomato slices on the bottom of 6 small bowls or molds. Strew with the ham slices. Place the herb sprigs over the ham and top each with a poached egg. Spoon the gelatin over the eggs. Chill for at least 1 hour. Dip each bowl briefly in hot water and unmold onto serving plates.

SERVES 6

Ragoût de Homard

[LOBSTER RAGOUT]

. . . .

LOBSTERS

1 CUP DRY WHITE WINE

3 QUARTS WATER

3 TABLESPOONS COARSE SALT

2 TEASPOONS BLACK
PEPPERCORNS

PINCH CAYENNE PEPPER

1 MEDIUM CARROT, QUARTERED

1 LEEK, TRIMMED AND CLEANED

1 BOUQUET GARNI (1 SPRIG
EACH THYME AND PARSLEY AND
1 BAY LEAF, TIED IN A SQUARE
OF CHEESECLOTH)

6 1- TO 1¼-POUND LIVE
LOBSTERS

. . . .

SAUCE

2 TABLESPOONS OLIVE OIL

2 MEDIUM ONIONS, JULIENNED

2 MEDIUM CARROTS, JULIENNED

1 LEEK, WHITE PART ONLY,
JULIENNED

4 TABLESPOONS COGNAC

1 CUP DRY WHITE WINE

3 MEDIUM TOMATOES, QUARTERED

4 GARLIC CLOVES, MINCED

1 BOUQUET GARNI (1 SPRIG
EACH THYME AND PARSLEY, AND
1 BAY LEAF, TIED IN A SQUARE
OF CHEESECLOTH)

1 SPRIG TARRAGON

4 CUPS WATER

SALT AND FRESHLY GROUND
PEPPER

PINCH CAYENNE PEPPER

3 TABLESPOONS ALL-PURPOSE
FLOUR, BLENDED WITH
2 TABLESPOONS SOFTENED
BUTTER

½ CUP CRÈME FRAÎCHE

. . . .

GARNISH

2 MEDIUM CARROTS, JULIENNED

2 MEDIUM TURNIPS, JULIENNED

1 LEEK, WHITE PART ONLY,
JULIENNED

½ POUND SMALL GREEN BEANS

TO PREPARE THE LOBSTERS: Combine all ingredients except the lobsters in a large pot. Bring to a boil and simmer for 10 minutes. Add the lobsters, boil for 8 minutes, then remove the lobsters and set aside.

Remove the lobster meat from the tails and set aside. Separate the claws and legs from the body and set aside. Cut up all the shells with kitchen scissors into small pieces. TO MAKE THE SAUCE: Heat 1 tablespoon of the olive oil in a large skillet and sauté the onions, carrots, and leek with the shells over medium-high heat for 3 minutes. Add 2 tablespoons of the cognac

BERNARD NOËL CREATES A MILDLY PIQUANT RAGOÛT DE HOMARD, A MÉLANGE OF
LOBSTER AND VEGETABLES.

. . . .

and flame with a match. Add the wine, tomatoes, garlic, bouquet garni, tarragon, water, salt and pepper, and cayenne. Bring to a boil and simmer for 30 minutes. Pour the sauce through a food mill into a medium saucepan. Return to heat and thicken the sauce by gradually whisking in the flour-butter mixture. Add the crème fraîche and set aside to keep warm.

TO MAKE THE GARNISH: Cook all of the julienned vegetables and beans in boiling salted water for 3 to 4 minutes, until tender-crisp. Drain and refresh in cold water.

Assemble the dish: Cut the reserved lobster tail meat into 1-inch pieces. Heat the remaining olive oil over medium-high heat in a large skillet. Add all of the reserved lobster pieces and vegetable garnish to the pan. Add the remaining cognac and flame with a match. Add the reserved sauce and bring to a simmer. Simmer for 2 minutes. Correct the seasoning.

To serve, arrange 2 claws and several legs on each of 6 plates and divide the lobster and vegetables onto each plate.

SERVES 6

Baba au Rhum

[RUM BABA]

. . . .

BABA

½ CUP MILK

1 ENVELOPE ACTIVE DRIED YEAST

½ TEASPOON SUGAR

1⅔ CUPS ALL-PURPOSE FLOUR

½ TEASPOON SALT

3 LARGE EGGS

5 TABLESPOONS UNSALTED BUTTER, SOFTENED

. . . .

RUM SYRUP

1 CUP SUGAR

1 CUP WATER

3 TABLESPOONS DARK RUM

. . . .

CHANTILLY CREAM

2 CUPS HEAVY CREAM

3 TABLESPOONS SUGAR

TO MAKE THE BABA: Scald the milk, then let cool to lukewarm. In an electric mixing bowl, combine the yeast, 1 tablespoon of hot water, the milk, sugar, and flour and beat until the dough is well combined. Beat in the salt. Beat in the eggs

one at a time to make a sticky dough. Continue beating the dough, adding the butter 1 tablespoon at a time. The dough should be smooth and silky, but still quite sticky. Sprinkle the top of the dough with flour, cover with a kitchen towel, and let rise until doubled, about one hour.

Preheat the oven to 400°F.

Butter an 8-cup ring mold. Stir down the dough with a wooden spoon and spread in the ring mold. Cover with a towel and let rise to the top of the mold, about 40 minutes. Bake for about 20 minutes, until golden brown. Remove from the oven and let cool for 5 minutes. Invert onto a rack over a pan.

TO MAKE THE SYRUP: Bring all of the ingredients to a boil in a small saucepan, stirring to dissolve the sugar. Let cool to lukewarm and pour over the warm cake. Excess syrup will drain into the pan. Continue to pour this syrup over the cake until it is absorbed.

TO MAKE THE CREAM: Whip the cream with the sugar. Serve the cake on a platter with the cream.

SERVES 10 TO 12

. . . .

AN EXTRA SPLASH OF RUM AT SERVING
TIME FINISHES A PERFECT BABA.

THE OLD DAYS OF LES HALLES ARE GONE, BUT THE BISTROS LIVE ON.

When the mood strikes for a true bistro meal, you have two options: to go directly to a true French bistro and indulge your mood to the limits of your appetite, or to prepare a bistro meal *chez vous,* using traditional recipes straight from the best bistro chefs and served on classic bistro dinnerware. On the following pages is a listing of sources—restaurants; bistroware supply houses; mail-order food emporiums, furniture, and antiques—to satisfy the bistro impulse whether you are in Paris or home by the range.

A GUIDE TO FEATURED PARIS BISTROS

L'Auberge Pyrénées-Cévennes (Chez Philippe)

106 Rue De La Folie-Mericourt,
Paris, 11th *arrondissement*
Tel.: 43-57-33-78.
Closed: Saturday and Sunday; the month of August. CARDS: VISA, MASTERCARD, AMEX.

. . . .

Benoît

20 rue Saint-Martin,
Paris, 4th *arrondissement*
Tel.: 42-72-25-76.
Closed: Saturday and Sunday; the month of August. CARDS: NONE.

. . . .

Le Bistro d'à Côté

10 rue Gustave-Flaubert,
Paris, 17th *arrondissement*
Tel.: 42-67-05-81.
Closed: Saturday and Sunday from April through August; Saturday lunch and Sunday in September.
CARDS: VISA, MASTERCARD.

. . . .

La Cafetière

21 rue Mazarine,
Paris, 6th *arrondissement*
Tel.: 46-33-76-90.
Closed: Sunday. CARDS: VISA, MASTERCARD.

. . . .

Chardenoux

1 rue Jules-Vallès,
Paris, 11th *arrondissement*
Tel.: 43-71-49-52.
Closed: Saturday lunch and Sunday; the month of August. CARDS: VISA, MASTERCARD, AMEX.

. . . .

Aux Charpentiers

10 rue Mabillon,
Paris, 6th *arrondissement*
Tel.: 43-26-30-05.
Closed: Sunday and holidays; the month of August. CARDS: VISA, MASTERCARD, AMEX, DINERS.

. . . .

D'Chez Eux

2 ave. Lowendal,
Paris, 7th *arrondissement*
Tel.: 47-05-52-55.
Closed: Sunday and holidays; the month of August. CARDS: VISA, MASTERCARD, AMEX.

. . . .

Au Chien Qui Fume

33 rue du Pont-Neuf
Paris, 1st *arrondissement*
Tel.: 42-36-07-42.
Open for lunch and dinner every day throughout the year. CARDS: VISA, MASTERCARD, AMEX, DINERS.

. . . .

La Fontaine de Mars

129 rue Saint-Dominique,
Paris, 7th *arrondissement*
Tel.: 47-05-46-44.
Closed: Saturday night and Sunday. CARDS: VISA, MASTERCARD.

. . . .

Chez Georges

273 Blvd. Pereire,
Paris, 17th *arrondissement*
Tel.: 45-74-31-00.
Open every day of the week; closed the month of August. CARDS: VISA, MASTERCARD.

. . . .

A L'Impasse

4 impasse Guéménée,
Paris, 4th *arrondissement*
Tel.: 42-72-08-45.
Closed: Saturday lunch, Sunday,
Monday dinner; the month of August. CARDS: VISA, MASTERCARD.

· · · · · · · · · ·

Le Petit Marguéry

9 Blvd. Port-Royal,
Paris, 13th *arrondissement*
Tel.: 43-31-58-59.
Closed: Sunday and Monday; the month of August. CARDS: VISA, MASTERCARD, AMEX, DINERS.

· · · · · · · · · ·

Polidor

41 rue Monsieur-le-Prince,
Paris, 6th *arrondissement*
Tel.: 43-26-95-34.
Open every day throughout the year until 1 A.M. CARDS: NONE.

· · · · · · · · · ·

Au Pont Marie

7 quai de Bourbon,
Paris, 4th *arrondissement*
(Ile-Saint-Louis)
Tel.: 43-54-79-62.

Closed: Saturday and Sunday;
August 15–September 1.
CARDS: NONE.

· · · · · · · · · ·

La Poule au Pot

9 rue Vauvilliers,
Paris, 1st *arrondissement*
Tel.: 42-36-32-96.
Open every day throughout the year from 7 P.M. until 6 A.M. only.
CARDS: VISA, MASTERCARD.

· · · · · · · · · ·

Le Restaurant Bleu

46 rue Didot,
Paris, 14th *arrondissement*
Tel.: 45-43-70-56.
Closed: Saturday and Sunday; the month of August. CARDS: NONE.

· · · · · · · · · ·

Restaurant de la Grille

80 rue du Faubourg Poissonnière,
Paris, 10th *arrondissement*
Tel.: 47-70-89-73.
Closed: Friday dinner, Saturday and Sunday; the month of August; and one week, February school vacation. CARDS: NONE

· · · · · · · · · ·

La Tour de Montlhéry (Chez Denise)

5 rue des Prouvaires,
Paris, 1st *arrondissement*
Tel.: 42-36-21-82.
Closed: Saturday and Sunday; mid-July–mid-August.
CARDS: VISA.

· · · · · · · · · ·

Le Vieux Bistro

14 rue du Cloître-Notre-Dame,
Paris, 4th *arrondissement*
(Ile-de-la-Cité)
Tel.: 43-54-18-95.
Open daily throughout the year.
CARDS: NONE.

· · · · · · · · · ·

OTHER RECOMMENDED PARIS BISTROS

Chez André

12 rue Marbeuf,
Paris, 8th *arrondissement*
Tel.: 47-20-59-57.
Closed: Tuesday; August 1–24.
CARDS: VISA, MASTERCARD.

· · · · · · · · · ·

Artois-Isidore

13 rue d'Artois,
Paris, 8th *arrondissement*
Tel.: 42-25-01-10.
Closed: Saturday lunch and Sunday. CARDS: VISA, MASTERCARD.

· · · · · · · · · ·

Le Brin de Zinc . . . et Madame

50 rue Montorgueil,
Paris, 1st *arrondissement*
Tel.: 42-21-10-80.
Closed: Saturday lunch, Sunday.
CARDS: VISA, MASTERCARD.

· · · · · · · · · ·

Aux Crus de Bourgogne

3 rue de Bachaumont,
Paris, 2nd *arrondissement*
Tel.: 42-33-48-24.
Closed: Saturday and Sunday; the month of August. CARDS: NONE.

· · · · · · · · · ·

Aux Fins Gourmets

213 Blvd. Saint-Germain,
Paris, 7th *arrondissement*
Tel.: 42-22-06-57.
Closed: Sunday; the month of August. CARDS: NONE.

Chez Georges

1 rue de Mail,
Paris, 2nd *arrondissement*
Tel.: 42-60-07-11.
Closed: Sunday and holidays.
CARDS: VISA, MASTERCARD, AMEX.

. . . .

La Gitane

53 bis Ave. de la Motte-Piquet,
Paris, 15th *arrondissement*
Tel.: 47-34-62-92.
Closed: Saturday and Sunday.
CARDS: VISA, MASTERCARD.

. . . .

Les Gourmets des Ternes

87 Blvd de Courcelles,
Paris, 17th *arrondissement*
Tel.: 42-27-43-04.
Closed: Saturday and Sunday; the month of August.
CARDS: VISA, MASTERCARD.

. . . .

La Hulotte

29 rue Dauphine,
Paris, 6th *arrondissement*

Tel.: 46-33-75-92.
Closed: Sunday and Monday; the month of August. CARDS: VISA, MASTERCARD, AMEX.

. . . .

Chez Maitre-Paul

2 rue Monsieur-le-Prince,
Paris, 6th *arrondissement*
Tel.: 43-54-74-59.
Closed: Sunday and Monday; the month of August; and one week at Christmas. CARDS: VISA, MASTERCARD, AMEX, DINERS.

. . . .

Pierre au Palais-Royal

10 rue de Richelieu,
Paris, 1st *arrondissement*
Tel.: 42-96-09-17.
Closed: Saturday, Sunday, and holidays; the month of August.
CARDS: VISA, MASTERCARD, AMEX.

. . . .

Chez Réné

14 Blvd. Saint-Germain,
Paris, 5th *arrondissement*
Tel.: 43-54-30-23.
Closed: Saturday and Sunday; the month of August. CARDS: NONE.

. . . .

Le Roi-du-Pot-au-Feu

34 rue Vignon,
Paris, 9th *arrondissement*
Tel.: 47-42-37-10.
Closed: Sunday.
CARDS: VISA, MASTERCARD.

. . . .

Chez la Vieille

1 rue Bailleul,
Paris, 1st *arrondissement*
Tel.: 42-60-15-78.
Open for lunch only. Closed: Saturday and Sunday; the month of August.

. . . .

MAIL-ORDER FOOD SPECIALTY SOURCES

Most bistro recipes call for only those ingredients available at any supermarket, but a few require more exotic items. Below are shops and producers who will mail-order unusual culinary supplies.

For domestic foie gras, confit of goose or duck, fresh ducks, goose fat, and a variety of prepared pâtés, terrines, entrees, and a free catalogue.

D'ARTAGNAN, INC.
399 St. Paul Avenue
Jersey City, N.J. 07306
Tel.: 201-792-0748
(Outside N.J.: 800-DARTAGAN)

For cheeses, foie gras, dried herbs, vinegars, oils, vanilla sugar, smoked salmon, caviar, truffles, lentils, preserves, chocolates, and charcuteries:

BALDUCCI'S
424 Avenue of the Americas
New York, N.Y. 10011
Tel.: 212-673-2600
(Outside N.Y.: 800-822-1444)

DEAN & DELUCA
560 Broadway
New York, N.Y. 10012
Tel.: 212-431-1691
Outside N.Y. City:
800-221-7714
(Also carries bistro dinnerware,
flatware and kitchen utensils;
catalogue available)

*For a broad range of domestic and
imported cheeses cut to order before
shipping:*

CHEESES OF ALL NATIONS
153 Chambers Street
New York, N.Y. 10007
Tel.: 212-732-0752
(Catalogue available for $1.00)

IDEAL CHEESE SHOP, LTD.
1205 Second Avenue
New York, N.Y. 10021
Tel.: 212-688-7579

*For a selection of goat cheese, fresh,
aged, or herbed:*

LITTLE RAINBOW CHEVRE
Box 379, Rodman Road
Hillsdale, N.Y. 12529
Tel.: 518-325-3351

*For smoked eastern and western
salmon:*

DUCKTRAP RIVER FISH FARM
RFD #2 Box 378
Lincolnville, Maine 04849
Tel.: 207-763-3960

*For live lobsters, fresh lobster meat,
shrimp, and sea scallops delivered
overnight:*

DOWNEAST SEAFOOD EXPRESS
Box 138
Brookville, ME 04617
Tel.: 800-556-2326

BISTROWARE SUPPLY HOUSES

The major Paris bistroware establishments do not offer mail-order
shopping. But when you are in
Paris, don't miss a visit to these
grand restaurant supply emporiums that stock an infinite variety
of glasses, sturdy dinnerware, flatware, carafes, bread baskets, fruit
baskets, egg baskets, mustard pots,
tureens, wine pitchers, sugar serv-
ers, espresso sets, salt and pepper
sets, candlesticks, coffeepots, soufflé dishes, butter dishes and pots,
cheese plates, escargot dishes and
holders, steak knives, copperware,
trays, cooking utensils, and even
menu holders, daily special black-
boards—everything you need to set
a bistro table or establish a bistro
kitchen.

VERRERIE DES HALLES
15 rue du Louvre
75001 Paris
Tel.: 42-36-86-02
Open Monday through Friday.

A. SIMON
36 rue Etienne-Marcel
Paris 75002
Tel.: 42-33-71-65
Open Monday through Saturday.

DEHILLERIN
18-20 rue Coquillière
75001 Paris
Tel.: 42-36-53-13
Open Monday through Saturday.

*For bistroware to buy or order in the
U.S., including glassware, dinnerware, ramekins, soufflé dishes, and
brioche molds:*

WILLIAMS-SONOMA
Mail Order Department
PO Box 7456
San Francisco, CA 94120-7456
Tel: 415-421-4242
(Merchandise available at more
than 90 Williams-Sonoma stores
across the United States)

BISTRO FURNITURE AND ANTIQUES

PIERRE DEUX, INC.
850 Madison Avenue
New York, N.Y. 10021
Tel.: 212-570-9343
(Wrought-iron bistro tables with
marble tops, wrought-iron bistro
chairs, and bar stools, to order.
Also available from Pierre Deux
shops across the U.S.)

T & K FRENCH ANTIQUES
120 Wooster Street
New York, N.Y. 10012
Tel.: 212-219-2472
FAX: 212-925-4876
(Classic woven-rattan café chairs
made to order in a wide choice of
color accents, woven rattan bar
stools, and wrought-iron bistro tables; also, antique bistro furniture.)